WAS SAGST DU?

KATE CORNEY

Thomas Nelson and Sons Ltd
Nelson House
Mayfield Road
Walton-on-Thames
Surrey
KT12 5PL
United Kingdom

© Kate Corney 1999

The right of Kate Corney to be identified as author of this work has been asserted by her in accordance with the Copyright, Design and Patents Act 1988.

First published by Thomas Nelson and Sons Ltd 1999
ISBN 0-17-440183-3
9 8 7 6 5 4 3 2 1
03 02 01 00 99

All rights reserved. No part of this publication may be reproduced, copied or transmitted in any form or by any means, electronic or mechanical, including photocopy, recording, or any information storage and retrieval system, without permission in writing from the publisher or under licence from the Copyright Licensing Authority Ltd, 90 Tottenham Court Road, London W1P 9HE.

Commissioning and development by Clive Bell.
Editorial by Marieke O'Connor.
Marketing by Michael Vawdrey.
Production by Gina Mance.
Illustrations by Chris Smedley.
Cover design by Eleanor Fisher.
Produced by Moondisks Ltd, Cambridge.
Printed in Spain by Grafo.

Acknowledgements

Thank you to the Northern Examinations and Assessment Board (NEAB) for permission to reprint their logos on page 71, and Marieke O'Connor for permission to reproduce the photograph on page 69.

The author and publishers would also like to thank Graham George, Subject Officer at AQA (NEAB), for his help with this title.

Contents

How to Do Well in Your Exam	4
Useful Phrases & the Alphabet	6
School (Foundation & Foundation/Higher Tier)	8
School (Higher Tier)	10
My Home (Foundation & Foundation/Higher Tier)	12
At Home (Foundation & Foundation/Higher Tier)	14
Home Life (Higher Tier)	16
Health and Fitness (Foundation & Foundation/Higher Tier)	18
Health and Fitness (Higher Tier)	20
Food (Foundation & Foundation/Higher Tier)	22
Food (Higher Tier)	24
Self, Family & Friends (Foundation & Foundation/Higher Tier)	26
Self, Family & Friends (Higher Tier)	28
Free Time & Special Occasions (Foundation & Foundation/Higher Tier)	30
Free Time & Special Occasions (Higher Tier)	32
Leisure & Arranging a Meeting (Foundation & Foundation/Higher Tier)	34
Leisure & Arranging a Meeting (Higher Tier)	36
Home Town & Customs (Foundation & Foundation/Higher Tier)	38
Home Town & Customs (Higher Tier)	40
Finding the Way (Foundation & Foundation/Higher Tier)	42
On the Road (Higher Tier)	44
Shopping (Foundation & Foundation/Higher Tier)	46
Shopping (Higher Tier)	48
Public Services (Foundation & Foundation/Higher Tier)	50
Public Services (Higher Tier)	52
Travel (Foundation & Foundation/Higher Tier)	54
Travel (Higher Tier)	56
Education & Employment (Foundation & Foundation/Higher Tier)	58
Education & Employment (Higher Tier)	60
Tourism (Foundation & Foundation/Higher Tier)	62
Tourism (Higher Tier)	64
Accommodation (Foundation & Foundation/Higher Tier)	66
Accommodation (Higher Tier)	68
Exam Practice for the Foundation Tier	70
Exam Practice for the Foundation/Higher Tier	72
Exam Practice for the Higher Tier	74
Numbers & Days	76
Months, Date & Question Words	77
German – English Glossary	78
English – German Glossary	79

How to Do Well in Your Exam

A Your Speaking Test

This book is all about helping you to do well in the role-play part of your GCSE Speaking Test. In the test, this is what will happen:

- If you are entered for Foundation Tier, your test will last 8–10 minutes.
- If you are entered for Higher Tier, your test will last 10–12 minutes.
- You will
  i begin with two role-plays
  ii give a short presentation which you have prepared in advance
  iii have a conversation with your teacher.
- Your own German teacher will carry out the Test which will be recorded on cassette.
- Your role-plays are worth one-third of the marks for the Speaking Exam and are therefore very important.
- You have about 10 minutes to prepare before your test, with your two role-play cards. It is a good idea to give yourself about eight minutes to prepare the role-plays and leave about two minutes to think about your presentation.

B What you need to learn

- The syllabus for your exam is based on various topics. In this book, you can learn all the German you need to talk about these topics.
- You can enter the exam at Foundation Tier or at Higher Tier.
- If you are entered at Foundation Tier, you need only learn and practise the language and tasks for Foundation Tier and Foundation/Higher Tier, for each topic in this book.
- If you are entered at Higher Tier, you must learn and practise all the language and tasks for every topic: this means that you need to work on all the pages of this book.

C How this book works

- This book is arranged in topics, the same as your exam syllabus.
- Each topic is divided into two parts:
  – Foundation Tier & Foundation/Higher Tier
  – Higher Tier
- Each part of each topic begins with a list of the key phrases you need to learn: see section **D** which gives you ideas about how to learn them.
- Beneath each list there is a cartoon: these cartoons help you to prepare for the conversations you may have in your Test, using the phrases in the list.
- On the page opposite the key phrases, you will find advice on how to prepare your role-plays and how to earn good marks. There are also practice role-plays which you can use to become really expert.

- On page 6 of this book, there is a list of important phrases which you can adapt to use in many topics. You will also find the alphabet on page 7. You must learn this really well as you will often be asked to spell something in your role-play.
- At the end of the book (pages 70–75), you will find some role-play tests which have been set in the exam: you can use these to revise everything you have learnt in this book and to prepare for your Speaking Test.
- On pages 76–80, there is a glossary of words you may need while working on this book, German to English and English to German. These pages also contain the German numbers, the days and months in German and question words.

D How you can learn the key phrases

- The main thing when trying to learn is to use your brain to do things which will help you to understand and remember these key phrases.
- The lists are divided into small sections: work on one section at a time and master those particular phrases before moving on to the next section.
- It is easier and quicker in the end to learn the phrases really well: if you only half learn them, you will soon forget them.
- Work in sessions of 15 to 20 minutes, with a gap between sessions. So, if you have a learning homework of 45 minutes, it is best to do 15 minutes, then take a break (do another subject, for example), do 15 more minutes followed by another break (listening to some music, for example) and then do a final session of 15 minutes.
- In each learning session, use two or three different learning activities. Here are some you can use:

1 Look at a phrase you are trying to learn and say it several times in your head. Then close your eyes and say it five more times. Finally, open your eyes and check that you were right.
2 Keep a piece of paper in this book, just less than the size of the pages. Cut out a section in the top right hand corner: it should be half of the page and about 4 cm deep, as shown:

> I play football.

a When you are starting to get to know the phrases in a section, cover the English with the piece of paper, look at the German and check that you can say the English for each phrase.

b Then cover the German and say or write all the German phrases to match the English.

c Gradually reveal the German phrases and see how quickly you can say what they are.
- You can do this from the top, e.g.

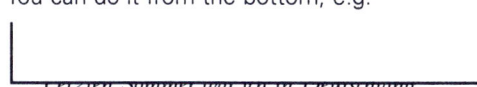

- You can do it from the bottom, e.g.

- And you can do it from the side, e.g.

Ich habe Zah|

d You can also cut a hole the size of a 10 pence coin in the middle of **your** piece of paper and move the hole around. You try to complete all the phrases that you see a part of, e.g.

3 Find ways to make the phrases your own, e.g.
a Change them to say what you want to say. If the phrase is *Mein Lieblingsfach ist Mathe*, change it to say what your favourite subject is.
b Make up conversations in your head, using the phrases and adapting them: write some of them down.

4 It often helps to work with a partner and it is especially useful to test each other to be sure that you really know the phrases, e.g.
a Partner A thinks of two phrases in the list. Partner B says six of the phrases and scores five points every time he/she says one of Partner A's phrases.
b Partner A reads all the questions in the list and Partner B answers them without looking at the list.
c Partner A asks Partner B to spell some key words, e.g. *Wie schreibt man das Wort Geschichte?*

d Partner A says a key word (as in the Higher Tier role-play cues) and Partner B says (from memory) a matching phrase from the list, e.g.
Partner A: Name.
Partner B: Ich heiße Susan.
Partner A: Geburtstag.
Partner B: Ich habe am fünften Mai Geburtstag.

5 A really good way to learn is to write some notes for all the phrases in a section. Then try to "photograph" the phrases in your mind. Cover up the phrases and use your notes to help you to write the phrases in full. Below are some ways of making these notes:
a Write the phrases and omit all the vowels, e.g.
Wir haben drei Schlafzimmer. Wr hbn dr Schlfzmmr
b Write the first letter only of each word, e.g.
Wir haben keine Garage.
W . . . h . . . k . . . G . . .
c Write the first and last words of each phrase, e.g.
Ich wohne in einem Doppelhaus.
Ich . . . . Doppelhaus.

6 It will help you a lot if you gradually increase the time gap between covering up the phrases and writing them. Start off with a gap of five minutes, then gradually increase the gap to 15 minutes, one hour, one day, one week.

7 Begin each learning session by quickly testing yourself on what you learnt in the last session. Find an activity which you used in the previous session and see if you can still do it. For example, cover the German phrases and say or write them from memory, looking at the English equivalents.

8 Before you start on a new topic, always revise one or two topics you learnt some time ago. This will help you to remember them for your exam and should also give you a pleasant surprise when you find out that you still know them!

Exam Tip
- The most important thing is to learn the key language really well. Then you will be able to use it correctly in your exam, and not only in the Role-plays. The language you learn in this book will also help you to do well in your Conversation and in your Writing Test. Just follow this advice as you work through the book and you should enjoy your role-playing and do really well in your exam.

5

Useful Phrases and the Alphabet

> **Exam Tip**
> • This is a list of phrases which you will use in many role-play topics. Learn them and they will help you to cope with all your role-plays.

I like …	*Ich mag …*
I like this pullover.	*Ich mag diesen Pullover.*
How do you like it?	*Wie gefällt dir das?*
I like it a lot.	*Es gefällt mir sehr.*
How did you like it?	*Wie hat es dir gefallen?*
I liked it.	*Es hat mir gut gefallen.*
What do you like to do?	*Was machst du gern?*
I like to …	*Ich … gern.*
I like to swim.	*Ich schwimme gern.*
I prefer to …	*Ich … lieber.*
I prefer to go to the cinema.	*Ich gehe lieber ins Kino.*
I would like …	*Ich möchte …*
I would like to go to the disco.	*Ich möchte in die Disco gehen.*
May I … ?	*Darf ich … ?*
May I phone my parents?	*Darf ich meine Eltern anrufen?*
I have to …	*Ich muss …*
I must be home at ten o'clock.	*Ich muss um zehn Uhr zu Hause sein.*
Can …	*Kann …*
What can you do here?	*Was kann man hier machen?*
Where can I buy stamps?	*Wo kann ich Briefmarken kaufen?*
Could you … ?	*Könnten Sie … ?*
Could you phone me back?	*Könnten Sie mich zurückrufen?*
I have …	*Ich habe …*
I have got a dog.	*Ich habe einen Hund.*
Have you … ?	*Hast du … ?*
Have you any brothers and sisters?	*Hast du Geschwister?*
Have you … ? (when talking to an adult)	*Haben Sie … ?*
Have you anything cheaper?	*Haben Sie etwas Billigeres?*
There is …	*Es gibt …*
There is a post office in the market place.	*Es gibt eine Post am Marktplatz.*
Is there … ?	*Gibt es … ?*
Is there another hotel nearby?	*Gibt es ein anderes Hotel in der Nähe?*
I am …	*Ich bin …*
I am sixteen.	*Ich bin sechzehn.*
Are you … ?	*Bist du … ?*
Are you tired?	*Bist du müde?*
How are you?	*Wie geht's?*
I am well.	*Es geht mir gut.*
I am not well.	*Es geht mir nicht gut.*
I am better.	*Es geht mir besser.*
My mother is better.	*Es geht meiner Mutter besser.*

It is …	*Es ist …*
It is interesting.	*Es ist interessant.*
It was …	*Es war …*
It was exciting.	*Es war spannend.*
I find …	*Ich finde …*
I find it boring.	*Ich finde es langweilig.*
How do I get … ?	*Wie komme ich … ?*
How do I get to the town centre?	*Wie komme ich zur Stadtmitte?*
I'll take …	*Ich nehme …*
I'll take these shoes.	*Ich nehme diese Schuhe.*
Let's meet …	*Treffen wir uns …*
Let's meet at my house.	*Treffen wir uns bei mir.*

Das Alphabet

> **Exam Tip**
> - You must learn how to say the letters of the alphabet in German. You will often be asked to spell your name or where you live. Practise these before your exam.

How do you write the address?	*Wie schreibt man den Straßennamen?*
Could you spell your name, please?	*Könnten Sie Ihren Namen bitte buchstabieren?*

A said like *ar* in car.
B said like the English word *bay*.
C said like *tsay*.
D said like the English word *day*.
E said like the letter A in English.
F said like *eff*.
G said like the English word *gay*.
H said like *ha*.
I said like the letter E in English.
J said like the English word *yacht*.
K said like the English word *car*.
L said like the letter L in English.
M said like the letter M in English.
N said like the letter N in English.
O said like *ow* in low.
P said like the English word *pay*.
Q said like *koo*.
R said like the English word *air*.
S said like the letter S in English.
T said like *tay*.
U said like *oo* in do.
V said like *fow* to rhyme with cow.
W said like *vay*.
X said like *iks*.
Y said like *üpsilon*.
Z said like *tset*.

School

Foundation Tier & Foundation/Higher Tier F&F/H

Die Fächer
Ich habe Mathe, Englisch …
Am Montag haben wir Deutsch.
Was ist dein Lieblingsfach?
Mein Lieblingsfach ist Sport.
Welche Fächer magst du gern?
Ich mag/mag nicht gern Geschichte.
Es ist interessant/einfach.
Magst du gern Erdkunde?
Ich finde Naturwissenschaften schwer.

School subjects
I do Maths, English …
On Monday, we have German.
What is your favourite subject?
My favourite subject is sport.
Which subjects do you like?
I like/don't like history.
It is interesting/easy.
Do you like geography?
I find science difficult.

Die Schule
Meine Schule gefällt mir sehr.
Sie ist modern/zu groß/zu klein.
Wie kommst du zur Schule?
Ich komme mit dem Rad/zu Fuß zur Schule.

School
I like my school a lot.
It is modern/too big/too small.
How do you come to school?
I come to school by bike/on foot.

Der Schultag
Wann beginnt die Schule?
Die erste Stunde beginnt um neun Uhr.
Wie viele Stunden hast du am Tag?
Wir haben fünf Stunden am Tag.
Wie lange dauert eine Stunde?
Eine Stunde dauert fünfzig Minuten.
Wann ist die Schule aus?
Die Schule ist um halb vier aus.
Was machst du in der Mittagspause?
Ich esse in der Kantine.
Ich spiele Fußball.

The school day
When does school begin?
The first lesson begins at nine o'clock.
How many lessons do you have a day?
We have five lessons a day.
How long does a lesson last?
A lesson lasts fifty minutes.
When does school end?
School ends at half past three.
What do you do in the lunch hour?
I eat in the canteen.
I play football.

Die Hausaufgaben
Ich mache meine Hausaufgaben.
Hast du viele Hausaufgaben?
Ich habe jeden Abend zwei Stunden Hausaufgaben.

Homework
I do my homework.
Do you have a lot of homework?
I have two hours homework each evening.

Du bist in einer deutschen Schule. Dein Freund stellt Fragen über deine Schule.

1. Work with your partner and practise reading the dialogue aloud. Partner A takes the part of the boy in the cartoon. Partner B closes the book and takes the part of the girl.
2. Swap roles. This time, Partner A closes the book and takes the part of the girl.

8

Foundation Tier & Foundation/Higher Tier F&F/H

Exam Practice

- In all the role-plays below, you are talking to a friend. Therefore you must use **du**.

 A
1 Complete this role-play.

Teacher's Role	Candidate's Role
1 Wann beginnt die Schule? 2 Wie viele Stunden hast du am Tag? 3 Wie lange dauert eine Stunde? 4 Und wann ist die Schule aus? 5 Das ist ein langer Tag!	1  2 4 3 70 min 4 

2 Now adapt the role-play to describe your school day.

 B
1 Look at the role-play below. Which task forces you to ask a question?
2 Work with your partner and complete the role-play.
3 Write out the role-play and learn the candidate's part.

Exam Tip
- You will always have to ask at least one question in your Foundation Tier role-play.
- Tasks which start with *Ask* ... always force you to ask a question, e.g. Ask if ... , Ask when ... , Ask where ... , Ask how ...

Teacher's Role	Candidate's Role
Du sprichst über deine Fächer. Ich bin dein Freund/deine Freundin. 1 Welche Fächer magst du gern? 2 Warum? 3 Ich finde Kunst schwer. 4 Ja, sehr. Es ist interessanter als Kunst. 5 Das ist schade.	You are talking to your German friend about your school subjects. 1 Say your favourite subject is art. 2 Say your teacher is interesting. 3 Ask if your friend likes music. 4 Say you find music boring. Your teacher will play the part of your friend and will speak first.

 C
1 In the role-play below, cover the teacher's role. Write a list of questions which your teacher could ask you for the ! task. Write an answer for each question in your list.
2 Uncover the teacher's role. Did you include the teacher's third question on your list?
3 Work with a partner and take it in turns to play the part of the candidate. Then write out the whole role-play and learn it.

Exam Tip
- In your Foundation/Higher Tier role-play, you will always see a !. This means your teacher will ask you an unexpected question. In the preparation time before your Speaking Test, try to work out what this question might be.

Teacher's Role	Candidate's Role
1 Wie kommst du normalerweise zur Schule? 2 Wie viele Stunden hast du vormittags? 3 Was machst du in der Mittagspause? 4 Du hast einen langen Tag. Hast du viele Hausaufgaben? 5 Du arbeitest aber fleißig!	Your German friend is talking to you about your school day. 1 Tell him/her how you get to school. 2 Tell him/her how many lessons you have each morning. 3 ! 4 Tell him/her how much homework you get. Your teacher will play the part of your friend and will speak first.

9

School

Higher Tier H

Die Fremdsprachen
Welche Fremdsprachen lernst du?
Ich lerne Deutsch und Französisch.
Seit wann lernst du Deutsch?
Ich lerne seit vier Jahren Deutsch.
Ich möchte Spanisch lernen.

Foreign languages
Which foreign languages do you learn?
I learn German and French.
How long have you been learning German?
I've been learning German for four years.
I'd like to learn Spanish.

Der Schultag
Welche Fächer hast du am Donnerstag?
Am Vormittag habe ich Informatik und Sport.

The school day
What subjects do you have on Thursday?
In the morning I have IT and sport.

Das Schuljahr
Ich besuche eine Gesamtschule/ein Gymnasium.
Wie viel Ferien hast du im Jahr?
Wir haben zu Weihnachten zwei Wochen Ferien.
Wir haben den ganzen Tag Schule.
Ich finde das deutsche Schulsystem besser.
Ich möchte lieber nur morgens Schule haben.
Unser Schultag ist zu lang und wir müssen dann abends die Hausaufgaben machen.

The school year
I go to a comprehensive school/a grammar school.
How many holidays do you have a year?
We have two weeks holiday at Christmas.
We have all day at school.
I find the German school system better.
I would prefer to have only morning school.
Our school day is too long and then we have to do homework in the evening.

Die Schuluniform
Wir müssen eine Schuluniform tragen.
Die Jungen tragen eine blaue Hose, ein weißes Hemd und eine gelbe Krawatte.
Die Mädchen tragen entweder einen Rock oder eine Hose.
Ich finde die Uniform langweilig, aber sie ist billig.

School uniform
We have to wear a school uniform.
The boys wear blue trousers, a white shirt and a yellow tie.
The girls wear either a skirt or trousers.
I find the school uniform boring, but it is cheap.

Die Schulregeln
Gibt es Schulregeln?
Wir dürfen in den Gängen nicht laufen.
Das finde ich aus Sicherheitsgründen richtig.
Wir dürfen im Klassenzimmer keinen Mantel tragen.
Das finde ich dumm, weil es im Klassenzimmer oft kalt ist.

School rules
Are there school rules?
We aren't allowed to run in the corridors.
I think that is right because it is safe.
We aren't allowed to wear coats in the classroom.
I find that stupid because it is often cold in the classroom.

Du sprichst über deine Schule.

1 Copy and complete the dialogue in the cartoons.
2 Work with a partner and practise acting out the dialogue.

10

Higher Tier H

Exam Practice

 A

In your Higher Tier role-play, each task will be indicated by a cue word. To prepare your role-play, read the English instructions and then prepare what you are going to say for each cue word. For example, if the cue word is *Beschreibung*, you will prepare a description of something. On the right are some cue words for the topic of "School". For each cue word, write as many sentences as possible.

Schultag   Schulsystem   Schulregeln
Mittagspause   Meinungen
Schuluniform   Schulferien
Hausaufgaben

Example Sprachen
- Ich lerne seit fünf Jahren Deutsch.
- Ich finde Deutsch einfacher als Französisch.

B

1 Cover the teacher's role and the model answer. Read the candidate's role. Prepare at least one sentence for each cue.
2 Now look at the teacher's role. Work with your partner and use your prepared answers to complete the whole role-play.
3 Write out the complete role-play without looking at the model dialogue.
4 Compare the model dialogue with your answer. Correct your answer if necessary and learn it.

Exam Tip
- In the Higher Tier role-play, you must complete each task and you must listen very carefully to what your teacher says to score high marks.
- You will have time to prepare your two role-plays before your Test. Take no more than four minutes for each role-play.
- Are you going to use *du* or *Sie* in this role-play? Why?

Teacher's Role

1 Musst du eine Schuluniform tragen?
   (*Candidate's task: to describe in detail the school uniform.*)
2 Was hältst du von der Uniform?
   (*Candidate's task: to state his/her opinion of the school uniform and to justify the opinion.*)
3 Was für Schulregeln gibt es in deiner Schule?
   (*Candidate's task: to state one school rule.*)
4 Gibt es eine Schulregel, die dich ärgert? Warum?
   (*Candidate's task: to describe a rule which annoys him/her and to say why it does.*)
5 Das finde ich auch dumm.

Candidate's Role

You are talking to your German friend about your school.
1 *Schuluniform*
2 *Meinung*
3 *Schulregeln*
4 *!*

Your teacher will play the part of your friend and will speak first.

Model Dialogue

– *Musst du eine Schuluniform tragen?*
– **Ja, ich trage einen blauen Rock, ein hellblaues Hemd und eine Krawatte.**
– *Was hältst du von der Uniform?*
– **Ich finde die Uniform ziemlich langweilig, aber sie ist nicht teuer und das ist gut.**
– *Was für Schulregeln gibt es in deiner Schule?*
– **Wir dürfen nicht ins Klassenzimmer gehen, bevor der Lehrer kommt.**
– *Gibt es eine Schulregel, die dich ärgert? Warum?*
– **Ja, wir müssen in der Pause immer draußen bleiben. Das finde ich dumm, weil es oft zu kalt ist.**
– *Das finde ich auch dumm.*

11

My Home

Foundation Tier & Foundation/Higher Tier

Haus oder Wohnung?
Wohnst du in einem Haus oder in einer Wohnung?
Ich wohne in einem Doppelhaus.
Meine Wohnung ist in der Stadtmitte.
Ich wohne in einem Dorf auf dem Land.
Ich wohne in einem großen Einfamilienhaus am Stadtrand.
Magst du dein Haus?
Ich mag mein Haus. Es ist sehr alt.
Wir haben einen kleinen Garten hinter dem Haus.
Wir haben keine Garage.

House or flat?
Do you live in a house or in a flat?
I live in a semi-detached house.
My house is in the town centre.
I live in a village in the country.
I live in a large detached house on the edge of town.
Do you like your house?
I like my house. It is very old.
We've got a small garden behind the house.
We have no garage.

Die Zimmer
Wie viele Zimmer hat das Haus?
Wir haben acht Zimmer.
Wir haben kein Esszimmer.
Wir essen in der Küche.
Wir haben eine Essecke im Wohnzimmer.
Wir haben drei Schlafzimmer und ein Badezimmer.
In der Küche gibt es eine Waschmaschine und einen Kühlschrank.
Es gibt einen Fernseher im Wohnzimmer und in meinem Zimmer.

The rooms
How many rooms does the house have?
We have eight rooms.
We have no dining-room.
We eat in the kitchen.
We have a dining area in the lounge.
We have three bedrooms and a bathroom.
In the kitchen, there is a washing machine and a fridge.
There is a television in the lounge and in my bedroom.

Mein Zimmer
Die Wände von meinem Zimmer sind grün und gelb.
Es gibt einen Kleiderschrank und einen Tisch in meinem Zimmer.
Gegenüber meinem Bett gibt es einen Fernseher.
Was machst du in deinem Zimmer?
Siehst du in deinem Zimmer fern?
Ich mache meine Hausaufgaben und ich sehe fern.

My room
My bedroom walls are green and yellow.
There is a wardrobe and a table in my bedroom.
Opposite my bed, there is a television.
What do you do in your bedroom?
Do you watch television in your bedroom?
I do my homework and I watch television.

Du sprichst über dein Haus.

1. Work with your partner and take it in turns to ask and answer the questions in the cartoon.
2. Copy out the dialogue in the cartoon, but change all the answers to describe where you live.

Foundation Tier &
Foundation/Higher Tier **F&F/H**

Exam Practice

 A

1 Take turns with your partner to complete the candidate's role below. Then write out the completed dialogue.
2 Now write a different answer for each task, by changing one detail, for instance: *Ich wohne in **einem Doppelhaus**.*

Teacher's Role	Candidate's Role
Du sprichst über dein Haus. Ich bin dein Freund/deine Freundin. 1 Wie viele Zimmer hast du? 2 Was gibt es in der Küche? 3 Was gibt es in deinem Zimmer? 4 Was machst du in deinem Zimmer? 5 Ich auch.	Your friend is asking you about your house. 1 Say there are nine rooms. 2 Say there is a dishwasher and a washing machine. 3 Say there is a bed and a table. 4 Say you read and watch television.

 B

1 Take it in turns with your partner to practise the candidate's role until you can complete the candidate's tasks from memory.
2 Write out the role-play and keep it for revision.

Exam Tip
• Spend only three minutes preparing the first role-play. There are more marks for the second role-play!
• Do not waste time checking words in dictionaries. Only use a dictionary if you really have to.

Teacher's Role	Candidate's Role
Du sprichst über dein Haus. Ich bin dein Freund/deine Freundin. 1 Wo wohnst du? 2 Wie viele Zimmer hat dein Haus? 3 Das ist schön. 4 Ich wohne auch in einem Haus. Hat dein Haus einen Garten? 5 Toll!	You are talking to your friend about your house. 1 Say you live in a terraced house in town. 2 Say you have four bedrooms. 3 Ask if your friend lives in a house or a flat. 4 Say you have a large garden behind the house. Your teacher will play the part of your friend and will speak first.

F/H **C**

1 In the role-play below, cover the teacher's role. What question do you think the teacher is going to ask you for your ! task?
2 Uncover the teacher's role. Did you guess the question correctly?
3 Write out the completed role-play.

Exam Tip
It is often quite easy to predict the ! task. In the preparation time before your Speaking Test, work out some questions and some answers to prepare yourself for the ! task.

Teacher's Role	Candidate's Role
1 Wo wohnst du genau? 2 Ist es ein großes Haus? 3 Das ist schön. Und was gibt es in deinem Zimmer? 4 Und was machst du in deinem Zimmer? 5 Ich auch.	You are talking with your German friend about your house. 1 Tell him/her that you live on the outskirts of town. 2 Tell him/her that you have four bedrooms. 3 Tell him/her that there is a bed, a cupboard and a television in your bedroom. 4 ! Your teacher will play the part of your friend and will speak first.

At Home

Foundation Tier & Foundation/Higher Tier F&F/H

Zu Hause helfen
Wie hilfst du zu Hause?
Ich mache mein Bett.
Ich räume mein Zimmer auf.
Am Wochenende bereite ich das Frühstück zu.
Manchmal wasche ich das Auto.
Letztes Wochenende habe ich im Garten gearbeitet.
Vor dem Essen decke ich den Tisch.
Nach dem Essen räume ich den Tisch ab.
Ich spüle und trockne ab.

Gast bei einer Familie
Was möchtest du jetzt machen?
Darf ich duschen?
Ich möchte baden.
Die Dusche ist gegenüber deinem Zimmer.
Ich möchte ins Bett gehen.
Wo ist die Toilette?
Hier neben meinem Zimmer.
Brauchst du etwas?
Hast du alles, was du brauchst?
Brauchst du einen Fön?
Ich habe kein Handtuch/keine Seife.
Wann ist Frühstück?
Wann essen wir?
Was machen wir morgen?
Wir gehen in die Stadt.
Abends essen wir gegen sieben Uhr.
Wir frühstücken gegen acht Uhr.

Helping at home
How do you help at home?
I make my bed.
I tidy my room.
At the weekend, I prepare breakfast.
Sometimes I wash the car.
Last weekend, I worked in the garden.
Before the meal, I set the table.
After the meal, I clear the table.
I wash up and dry the dishes.

Staying with a family
What would you like to do now?
May I have a shower?
I would like to have a bath.
The shower is opposite your bedroom.
I would like to go to bed.
Where is the toilet?
Here, next to my bedroom.
Do you need anything?
Have you got everything you need?
Do you need a hairdryer?
I haven't got a towel/any soap.
When is breakfast?
When are we going to eat?
What are we going to do tomorrow?
We are going to town.
In the evening, we eat at about seven o'clock.
We have breakfast at about eight o'clock.

Du hast Besuch aus Deutschland.

1. Use the pictures to write out the completed dialogues from the cartoons.
2. Practise the completed dialogues with your partner.

Exam Tip
- In your exam, if you don't know the German for "toothpaste" you will have to look it up in a dictionary. For the moment you can use the glossary at the back of this book.

Foundation Tier & Foundation/Higher Tier

Exam Practice

 A

Write a question in German for each task below.
1 Ask what your friend does to help at home.
2 Ask if your friend needs a towel.
3 Ask what your friend would like to do.
4 Ask when you are going to have lunch.
5 Ask if you can have a bath.
6 Ask what you are going to do tomorrow.

> *Exam Tip*
> - In the role-plays below, you are talking to a friend. Will you use *du* or *Sie*?
> - What would you use if the role-play instructions said that you were talking to an adult who was staying with you?

 B

1 Practise this role-play with your partner. Then write it out and learn it.

Teacher's Role	Candidate's Role
Dein deutscher Freund/deine deutsche Freundin wohnt bei dir. Ich bin dein Freund/deine Freundin. 1 Wann ist Frühstück? 2 Darf ich duschen? 3 Danke schön. 4 Das wäre nett. Was machen wir morgen? 5 Toll!	Your German friend is staying with you. 1 Say breakfast is at about 8 o'clock. 2 Say the bathroom is opposite your friend's room. 3 Ask if your friend needs a hairdryer. 4 Say you are going to school tomorrow. Your teacher will play the part of your friend and will speak first.

2 Now work with a partner to create a new role-play by changing one thing in each of the candidate's English tasks.
   Example
   Say breakfast is at about 8.30.
3 Work with your partner and practise your new role-plays.

 C

1 Cover the teacher's role and the model dialogue. Take four minutes only to prepare the candidate's tasks.
2 Uncover the teacher's role. Write out your completed role-play, then compare your answer with the model dialogue.

Teacher's Role	Candidate's Role
1 Ich möchte helfen. Wie hilfst du abends zu Hause? 2 Wann isst du normalerweise zu Abend? 3 Was machen wir morgen? 4 Das ist schön. Darf ich vor dem Abendessen duschen? 5 Danke.	Your German friend is staying with you. 1 Tell him/her what you do to help at home in the evening. 2 Tell him/her that you normally eat at seven but that this evening you are going to eat at eight o'clock. 3 ! 4 Tell him/her exactly where the bathroom is. Your teacher will play the part of your friend and will speak first.

Model Dialogue

– Ich möchte helfen. Wie hilfst du abends zu Hause?
– **Ich decke den Tisch und spüle ab.**
– Wann isst du normalerweise zu Abend?
– **Wir essen normalerweise um sieben Uhr aber heute abend essen wir um acht Uhr.**
– Was machen wir morgen?
– **Wir gehen in die Schule und dann gehen wir in die Stadt.**
– Das ist schön. Darf ich vor dem Abendessen duschen?
– **Ja, das Badezimmer ist hier links neben deinem Zimmer.**
– Danke.

Home Life

Higher Tier H

Das Essen
Mittags essen wir normalerweise warm.
In der Woche esse ich um zwölf Uhr dreißig zu Mittag.
Abends bereitet meine Mutter etwas Warmes vor.
Am Sonntag essen wir normalerweise einen Braten.
Ich esse fast kein Frühstück, weil ich keine Zeit habe.
Ich mag das Frühstück am Sonntag am liebsten.
Am Sonntag habe ich Zeit und dann esse ich viel.

Meals
At lunch-time, we normally have a hot meal.
During the week, I eat lunch at twelve thirty.
In the evening, my mother prepares a hot meal.
On Sunday, we normally have a roast.
I eat hardly any breakfast because I don't have time.
My favourite meal is breakfast on Sunday.
On Sunday, I have time and then I eat a lot.

Zu Hause helfen
Wie kann ich dir helfen?
Könntest du bitte den Tisch decken?
Könntest du bitte abspülen?
Könntest du bitte einkaufen gehen?
Das ist nett von dir, aber es gibt nichts zu tun.
Ich habe schon abgespült.
Du könntest uns im Garten helfen.
Wir müssen alle zu Hause helfen, weil meine Mutter berufstätig ist.
Meine Mutter bereitet oft das Essen zu.
Mein Bruder räumt immer sein Zimmer auf.
Meine Schwester hilft nicht viel. Sie ist sehr faul.
Gestern habe ich im Garten geholfen.

Helping at home
How can I help you?
Could you please set the table?
Could you please wash up?
Could you please go shopping?
That's kind of you but there isn't anything to do.
I have already washed up.
You could help us in the garden.
We all have to help at home because my mother has a job.
My mother often prepares the meals.
My brother always tidies his room.
My sister doesn't help much. She is very lazy.
Yesterday, I helped in the garden.

Mein Zimmer
Zum Glück habe ich mein eigenes Zimmer.
Ich teile ein Zimmer mit meiner Schwester/meinem Bruder.
Ich möchte lieber mein eigenes Zimmer haben.

My room
Luckily, I have my own room.
I share a room with my sister/my brother.
I would like to have my own room.

Dein deutscher Freund wohnt bei dir.

1. Work with a partner and practise reading aloud the dialogue above.
2. Copy the three questions from the dialogue. Close your book and try to answer the questions.

Higher Tier H

Exam Practice

A

1 Complete the gapped dialogues below.
2 Work with a partner. Partner A closes the book. Partner B asks him/her the questions from the two dialogues. Partner A makes up a new answer to each question. Then swap roles. How many different answers can you make?

Dialog 1
Also, wie kann ich deinen Eltern helfen?
....
Kann ich auch nach dem Essen helfen?
....
Hilft dein Bruder viel zu Hause?
....
Wer arbeitet im Garten?
....

Dialog 2
Hier ist dein Zimmer. Hast du auch zu Hause dein eigenes Zimmer?
....
Wie gefällt dir das?
....
Was isst man normalerweise hier zum Frühstück?
....
Und wer bereitet das Frühstück vor?
....

B

1 Cover the teacher's role and the model dialogue. Prepare the candidate's role. Remember to try to predict what question your teacher might ask you when you see !.
2 Now look at the teacher's role. Did you predict the question correctly? Write out the complete role-play.

Teacher's Role

1 Wann und wo isst du normalerweise am Sonntag zu Mittag? *(Candidate's task: to say when and where he/she normally eats lunch.)*
2 Und was isst du normalerweise am Sonntag? *(Candidate's task: to say what they eat for lunch on Sunday – four details needed.)*
3 Wie hilfst du, das Essen vorzubereiten? *(Candidate's task: to give two ways in which he/she helps.)*
4 Was ist deine Lieblingsmahlzeit? Warum? *(Candidate's task: to state favourite meal and to justify his/her choice.)*
5 Ich auch.

Candidate's Role

Your German friend is staying with you. You are talking about meals.
1 *Mittagessen*
2 *Sonntagsessen*
3 *!*
4 *Lieblingsmahlzeit*

Your teacher will play the part of your friend and will speak first.

3 Read the model dialogue and compare it with your answer.
4 Change all the underlined words in the answer to write a new role-play.

Model Dialogue

– Wann und wo isst du normalerweise am Sonntag zu Mittag?
– **Wir essen normalerweise am Sonntag zu Hause. Wir essen gegen zwei Uhr.**
– Und was isst du normalerweise am Sonntag?
– **Wir essen oft Hähnchen mit Kartoffeln und Erbsen. Zum Nachtisch essen wir eine Torte mit Sahne.**
– Wie hilfst du, das Essen vorzubereiten?
– **Ich wasche die Kartoffeln und nach dem Essen räume ich den Tisch ab.**
– Was ist deine Lieblingsmahlzeit? Warum?
– **Ich mag am liebsten das Mittagessen am Sonntag, weil wir immer so viel essen.**
– Ich auch.

Health & Fitness

Foundation Tier & Foundation/Higher Tier F&F/H

Was ist los?	**What is wrong?**
Wie geht's?	How are you?
Es geht./Es geht mir nicht gut./Es geht mir besser.	I am well./I don't feel well./I feel better.
Hilfe!	Help!
Was ist los?	What's wrong?
Ich bin krank.	I am ill.
Was fehlt dir?	What's the matter with you?
Ich habe Durst.	I am thirsty.
Ich habe keinen Hunger.	I am not hungry.
Mir ist kalt/heiß/Ich habe Fieber.	I am cold/hot/I've got a temperature.
Was soll ich machen?	What should I do?
Was möchtest du machen?	What would you like to do?
Ich möchte mich hinlegen.	I would like to lie down.
Hast du Tabletten?	Have you got any tablets?
Ich möchte bitte ein Glas Wasser.	I'd like a glass of water, please.
Wann kann ich den Arzt sprechen?	When can I see the doctor?
Wo tut es weh?	**Where does it hurt?**
Kannst du mir helfen?	Can you help me? (talking to a friend)
Können Sie mir helfen?	Can you help me? (talking to an adult)
Ich habe Zahnschmerzen/einen Schnupfen/Durchfall.	I've got toothache/a cold/diarrhoea.
Ich habe Kopfschmerzen/Halsschmerzen.	I've got a headache/a sore throat.
Du hast vielleicht Grippe.	Perhaps you have 'flu.
Mein Bein tut weh.	My leg hurts.
Seit wann hast du das?	How long have you had it?
Seit drei Stunden/seit zwei Tagen/seit gestern.	For three hours/for two days/since yesterday.
Du sollst dich hinlegen.	You should lie down.

Du wohnst bei einer deutschen Familie. Eines Tages geht es dir nicht gut.

1. Practise dialogue **A** with your partner.
2. Cover dialogue **A** and complete dialogue **B**.

Exam Practice

A

It is important to be able to ask and answer questions in your role-play.

Read the list of questions below and then the list of answers. Copy each question together with its matching answer. One question has no answer. Write your answer to that question.

1 Wie geht's?
2 Was ist los?
3 Was fehlt dir?
4 Seit wann hast du das?
5 Was möchtest du machen?
6 Hast du Tabletten?
7 Wann kann ich den Arzt sprechen?
8 Was soll ich machen?

a Ich möchte mich hinlegen.
b Ich kann ihn jetzt anrufen.
c Es geht.
d Ja, natürlich.
e Du sollst dich hinlegen.
f Ich bin krank.
g Ich habe Durchfall.

B

1 Use three minutes only to prepare the role-play below.
2 As soon as you have used your three minutes, work with a partner and complete the role-play, taking turns to complete the candidate's role.
3 Write out the completed role-play.

Teacher's Role

Du wohnst bei deinem Freund/deiner Freundin in Österreich. Ich bin dein Freund/deine Freundin.
1 Du siehst blass aus.
2 Was ist los?
3 Seit wann hast du das?
4 Das ist bestimmt nichts Ernstes.
5 Ich hole dir Tabletten.

Candidate's Role

You are staying with your friend in Austria.

1 Say you are ill.
2 Say you have a sore throat.
3 Say how long you have had it.
4 Ask what you should do.

Your teacher will play the part of your friend and will speak first.

(Adapted from AQA/NEAB – 1998)

C

1 Take four minutes to prepare the role-play.
2 Practise with your partner.
3 Write out the completed role-play and underline any parts which you found difficult. Concentrate on these when you learn the role-play.

Exam Tip
- The ! task in this role-play asks the candidate to spell his/her name.
- This is a very popular question. Make sure you recognise the question which can be either: *Wie schreibt man das?* or *Kannst du das buchstabieren?*
- Make sure that you can spell your name correctly and without too much hesitation.

Teacher's Role

1 Guten Morgen.
2 Was fehlt Ihnen?
3 Leider ist der Arzt heute nicht frei.
4 Ich werde mit dem Arzt sprechen. Wie heißen Sie? Wie schreibt man das?
5 Danke. Nehmen Sie bitte Platz.

Candidate's Role

You are at the doctor's in Austria.
1 Ask when you can see the doctor.
2 Explain what the matter is.
3 Ask what you should do.
4 !

Your teacher will play the part of the receptionist and will speak first.

(AQA/NEAB – 1998)

Health & Fitness

Higher Tier H

Einen Termin veranstalten
Ich habe mich beim Zahnarzt angemeldet.
Ich möchte einen Termin beim Arzt.
Wann kann ich den Arzt sprechen, bitte?
Wann möchten Sie kommen?
Ich brauche einen Termin für heute Abend.
Ich muss heute kommen. Ich fahre morgen nach Hause.
Ich brauche vor der Reise Tabletten.
Ich habe furchtbare Zahnschmerzen.

Making an appointment
I've got an appointment with the dentist.
I would like an appointmant with the doctor.
When can I see the doctor, please?
When would you like to come?
I need an appointment for this evening.
I must come today. I'm going home tomorrow.
I need tablets before I travel.
I've got terrible toothache.

Fragen stellen
Ich habe einen Sonnenbrand. Was können Sie mir empfehlen?
Mir ist schlecht.
Wann und wie oft soll ich die Tabletten nehmen?
Sie nehmen die Tabletten viermal am Tag vor dem Essen.
Ich bin hingefallen.
Ich habe mir den Fuß verletzt.
Ich habe mir den Arm verbrannt.
Ich habe mir in den Finger geschnitten.

Asking questions
I'm sunburnt. What can you recommend?
I feel sick.
When and how often should I take the tablets?
You take the tablets four times a day before meals.
I have fallen over.
I have hurt my foot.
I have burnt my arm.
I have cut my finger.

Gesund leben
Ich treibe viel/nicht genug Sport.
Ich esse zu oft Pommes.
Ich gehe während der Woche früh ins Bett.
Ich habe so viele Hausaufgaben, dass ich oft spät ins Bett gehen muss.
Ich versuche, jeden Tag viel Obst zu essen.
Ich mache jedes Wochenende eine Wanderung.

Healthy living
I do a lot/not enough sport.
I eat chips too often.
I go to bed early during the week.
I have so much homework that I often have to go to bed late.
I try to eat a lot of fruit each day.
I go for a walk each weekend.

Du wohnst in Österreich. Eines Tages geht es dir nicht gut.

Complete the answers in the dialogue above and write out the whole dialogue. Then work with a partner. Take it in turns to ask and answer the questions.

Du sprichst mit deiner österreichischen Freundin über Sport.

Copy and complete the dialogue above. The pictures in the think bubbles will help you to answer the girl's questions.

20

Higher Tier H

Exam Practice

H A

1 In your Higher Tier role-play, each task will be indicated by a cue word. Which candidate's utterance below matches which cue?

Cue	Candidate
1 Sport	a Ich habe Durchfall.
2 Zahnarzt	b Ich esse viel Gemüse.
3 Schlaf	c Ich möchte den Zahnarzt sprechen.
4 Was fehlt?	d Ich treibe viel Sport.
5 Essen	e Ich gehe nicht früh ins Bett.

2 Each candidate's utterance above is short. Sometimes your teacher will ask you to give more than one detail and will ask you an extra question. What could you add to each utterance above to give an extra detail?

Example

*Ich habe Durchfall **und mir ist schlecht***.

H B

1 Revise pages 18 and 20 and make sure you know all the key phrases.
2 Cover up the teacher's role below, and give yourself just four minutes to prepare this role-play. Remember to think of questions the teacher could ask you for the ! task.

Teacher's Role

1 Kann ich Ihnen helfen?
2 Was fehlt Ihnen?
3 Sie können den Arzt morgen Abend sprechen. Geht das?
4 Warum muss es heute sein?
5 Ich werde mal mit dem Arzt sprechen.

Candidate's Role

You have fallen over and hurt your arm. You want to see a doctor before you travel home tomorrow.

1 *Arzt*
2 *Was fehlt?*
3 *Wann*
4 *!*

Your teacher will play the part of the doctor's receptionist and will speak first.

---

3 Practise the role-play with your partner.
4 Write out your completed role-play and compare it with the model dialogue below.

Model Dialogue

– Kann ich Ihnen helfen?
– **Ich möchte den Arzt sprechen.**
– Was fehlt Ihnen?
– **Ich bin hingefallen und ich habe mir den Arm verletzt.**
– Sie können den Arzt morgen Abend sprechen. Geht das?
– **Nein, ich muss heute kommen.**
– Warum muss es heute sein?
– **Ich fahre morgen nach Hause und ich brauche vor der Reise Tabletten.**
– Ich werde mal mit dem Arzt sprechen.

5 Using the pictures next to the candidate's cues below, adapt the role-play above.

Candidate's Role

You have very bad toothache and want to see a dentist this evening.

1 *Zahnarzt*
2 *Was fehlt?*
3 *Wann?* 20:00
4 *!*

Your teacher will play the part of the dentist's receptionist and will speak first.

Food

Foundation Tier & Foundation/Higher Tier F&F/H

Zu Hause essen
Möchtest du jetzt etwas Käse?
Nein, danke. Ich esse nicht gern Käse.
Noch etwas Suppe?
Ja, gern. Die Suppe schmeckt sehr gut.
Isst du gern Hähnchen?
Leider nicht. Ich esse kein Fleisch.
Ich esse sehr gern Fisch.
Ich trinke gern Apfelsaft.
Das war lecker.
Gib mir das Salz, bitte.
Ich brauche einen Löffel.

Eating at home
Would you like some cheese now?
No, thank you. I don't like cheese.
Some more soup?
Yes, please. The soup tastes very good.
Do you like chicken?
Unfortunately not. I don't eat meat.
I like fish very much.
I like apple juice.
That was delicious.
Pass me the salt, please.
I need a spoon.

Im Restaurant und Café essen
Herr Ober! /Fräulein!
Bitte sehr?
Die Speisekarte, bitte.
Einmal Tomatensuppe.
Zweimal Bratwurst mit Pommes.
Ich möchte ein Glas Mineralwasser.
Noch ein Bier, bitte.
Als Nachtisch möchte ich ein Stück Erdbeertorte.
Haben Sie Eis?
Was für Kuchen haben Sie?
Ich möchte das Menü für DM 15, bitte.
Was ist Schwarzwälder Kirschtorte?
Das ist eine Art Kuchen mit Schokolade und Kirschen.
Wo ist die Toilette, bitte?
Zahlen, bitte.

Eating in a restaurant and café
(You say this to call the waiter/waitress.)
Can I help you?
The menu, please.
One tomato soup.
Two sausage and chips.
I would like a glass of mineral water.
Another beer, please.
For dessert, I would like a piece of strawberry tart.
Do you have ice cream?
What sort of cakes have you got?
I'd like the DM 15 menu, please.
What is Black Forest gateau?
It is a kind of cake with chocolate and cherries.
Where is the toilet, please?
The bill, please.

Du bist in einem Restaurant in der Schweiz.

1 Work with your partner and practise reading the dialogue aloud.
2 With your partner, make up a new dialogue by changing the underlined words.

B
- Champignonschnitzel = Schweinefleisch mit Champignonsoße.

Look at this receipt. Write out a conversation in which a customer orders the items on the receipt. Base your conversation on the dialogue in cartoon A.

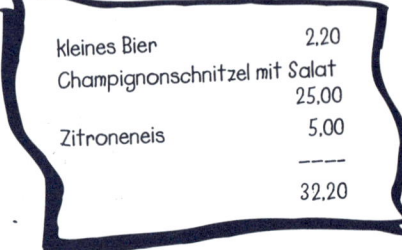

22

Exam Practice

Foundation Tier & Foundation/Higher Tier F&F/H

F A

1 Take three minutes to prepare the role-play below. Practise the role-play with your partner and write out the completed role-play.
2 Change the candidate's utterances to say what you like to eat and to ask for something you might need at the table.

> *Exam Tip*
> - Be careful with the role-plays in this topic. If you are talking to a friend when you are eating at home, use *du*.
> - If you are talking to an adult, perhaps one of your friend's parents or a waiter/waitress, use *Sie*.

Teacher's Role

Du isst bei deinem Freund/bei deiner Freundin.
1 Was für Fleisch isst du gern?
2 Isst du gern Gemüse?
3 Kein Problem. Wie schmeckt dir die Torte?
4 Das freut mich.
5 Gern.

Candidate's Role

You are having a meal with your German friend.
1 Say you like chicken.
2 Say you don't like peas.
3 Say it is delicious.
4 Ask your friend to pass the sugar.

Your teacher will play the part of your friend and will speak first.

F B

Now prepare this role-play in three minutes. Try not to use the glossary at the back.

Teacher's Role

Du bist in einem Restaurant in der Schweiz. Ich bin der Kellner/die Kellnerin.
1 Guten Tag.
2 Bitte sehr.
3 Ja, gern.
4 Bitte sehr. Und zu trinken?
5 Kommt sofort.

Candidate's Role

You are in a restaurant in Switzerland.
1 Ask if there is a tourist menu.
2 Ask for tomato soup.
3 Ask for chicken and salad.
4 Ask for a bottle of mineral water.

Your teacher will play the part of the waiter or waitress and will speak first.

(Adapted from AQA/NEAB – 1998)

C

1 In this topic, the teacher could ask you several questions when you see a ! task.
   Copy the questions below and write an answer for each question.
   a Bitte sehr?
   b Was möchten Sie trinken?
   c Und zu essen?
   d Was für Gemüse möchten Sie?
   e Hätten Sie gern einen Nachtisch?
2 In the role-play below, cover the teacher's role and try to predict the ! question and prepare your answer.
3 Write out the role-play and learn it.

Teacher's Role

1 Guten Tag. Bitte sehr?
2 Was möchten Sie trinken?
3 Hier ist die Getränkekarte.
4 Bitte sehr. Was möchten Sie als Nachtisch?
5 Sehr gern.

Candidate's Role

You are in a restaurant in Austria.
1 Order something warm to eat.
2 Ask what sort of drinks they have.
3 Say you would like a glass of white wine and an orange juice for your friend.
4 !

Your teacher will play the part of the waiter or waitress and will speak first.

Food

Higher Tier H

Über das Essen sprechen	Talking about food
Ich möchte etwas Gesundes essen.	I would like something healthy to eat.
Ich möchte lieber etwas typisch Deutsches essen.	I would prefer something typically German.
Ich möchte österreichische Spezialitäten probieren.	I would like to try some Austrian specialities.
Ich bin Vegetarier(in).	I am a vegetarian.
Ich esse sehr gern italienische Spezialitäten, besonders Pizza.	I like Italian specialities very much, especially pizza.
Noch etwas Fisch?	Some more fish?
Das war wirklich lecker, aber das reicht.	That was really delicious but I've had enough.
Das hat besonders gut geschmeckt, aber nur ein bisschen, bitte.	That tasted especially good, but just a little, please.
Ich habe schon so viel gegessen.	I have already eaten so much.
Noch einige Kartoffeln?	Some more potatoes?
Ja, bitte. Sie schmecken sehr gut.	Yes, please. They taste very good.
Ich bin gegen Eier allergisch.	I am allergic to eggs.
Ich habe diese Torte noch nie probiert.	I have never tried this gateau.
Sagen Sie dem Koch, es war sehr gut.	Please tell the cook it was very good.
Vielen Dank für ein wunderbares Essen.	Thank you very much for a wonderful meal.
Möchtest du Zucker?	Would you like some sugar?
Brauchen Sie ein Messer?	Do you need a knife?

Einen Tisch reservieren	Reserving a table
Wie viele sind Sie denn?	How many are you?
Wir möchten einen Tisch für vier Personen.	We would like a table for four people.
Ich habe einen Tisch am Fenster reserviert.	I have reserved a table in the window.
Haben Sie auf der Terrasse einen Tisch für drei?	Have you got a table on the terrace for three?
Ich möchte einen Nichtrauchertisch für morgen Abend reservieren.	I would like to reserve a non-smoking table for tomorrow evening.
Können wir im Schatten sitzen?	Can we sit in the shade?

Probleme	Problems
Die Zwiebelsuppe hat schrecklich geschmeckt. Sie war kalt!	The onion soup tasted awful. It was cold!
Ich warte schon seit einer halben Stunde.	I have already been waiting half an hour.
Ich möchte mit dem Oberkellner sprechen.	I would like to speak to the manager.
Ich habe Omelett und keinen Fisch bestellt.	I ordered omelette, not fish.

Zahlen	Paying
Ist das inklusive Bedienung?	Is service included?
Ist der Wein im Menü einbegriffen?	Is wine included in the fixed-price menu?

Du möchtest in einem Restaurant zu Mittag essen.

Practise the dialogue above with a partner. Then write a new dialogue. This time, you want to reserve a no-smoking table for two people, at the window.

Higher Tier H

Exam Practice

H **A**

1 To help you to predict the question your teacher will ask you when you see a ! task, think of questions which go with the topic and setting. Copy the questions below and write an answer for each.

You are having a meal with a German family.

2 Now write your own questions and answers to match the following topics and settings:
   a You phone a restaurant to reserve a table.
   b You are talking with your German friend about food.

H **B**

> *Exam Tip*
> - Whenever you are asked to make a suggestion or to express an opinion in your Higher Tier role-play, you will always have to follow it with a reason.
> - In your second task, you need to describe the sort of restaurant you want to visit. You do not need to give a name.
> - The third task asks you to give details of the restaurant. Keep it simple, but give more than one detail. Remember that you have already given one detail when you gave a reason for your choice. You cannot use the same detail again.
> - The unexpected question does not come from this same topic of "Eating in a Restaurant". Be prepared for this. Examiners often combine more than one topic in a role-play.

1 Cover the teacher's role and the model dialogue and prepare the role-play.
2 With the help of the teacher's role, complete the role-play. Then look at the model dialogue. Notice how the candidate uses simple details to complete the third task.

Teacher's Role	**Candidate's Role**
1 Ich möchte gern ins Restaurant gehen, um Steak zu essen. *(Candidate's task: to disagree about going for a steak and give a reason.)* 2 Wo möchtest du sonst essen? Warum? *(Candidate's task: to suggest another place to eat and say why he/she prefers to go there.)* 3 Klasse! Warum gefällt dir dieses Restaurant sonst noch? *(Candidate's task: to say what he/she likes about the place.)* 4 Also, dann gehen wir dorthin. Wann sollen wir gehen? Wie kommen wir zum Restaurant? *(Candidate's task: to suggest when to go and how to get there.)*	Your German friend is staying with you. You want to go out for a meal, but you do not eat meat. 1 *deine Meinung* 2 *Vorschlag* 3 *Details des Restaurants* 4 ! Your teacher will play the part of your friend and will speak first.

(Adapted from AQA/NEAB – 1998)

Model Dialogue
– *Ich möchte gern ins Restaurant gehen, um Steak zu essen.*
– **Ich leider nicht. Ich esse kein Fleisch.**
– *Wo möchtest du sonst essen? Warum?*
– **Gehen wir lieber in ein Fischrestaurant. Ich esse sehr gern Fisch und du isst auch gern Fisch, oder?**
– *Klasse! Warum gefällt dir dieses Restaurant sonst noch?*
– **Es ist billig und man kann dort wunderbare Torten essen.**
– *Also, dann gehen wir dorthin. Wann sollen wir gehen? Wie kommen wir zum Restaurant?*
– **Sollen wir um acht gehen? Es ist nicht weit. Wir können zu Fuß gehen.**

Self, Family & Friends

Foundation Tier & Foundation/Higher Tier F&F/H

Ich / Me

Ich heiße …	I am called …
Wie schreibt man das?/Wie alt bist du?	How do you write that?/How old are you?
Ich bin sechzehn.	I am sixteen.
Wann hast du Geburtstag?	When is your birthday?
Ich habe am vierundzwanzigsten Mai Geburtstag.	My birthday is on May 24th.
Ich wohne in ………/Ich komme aus England/Schottland.	I live in ……/I come from England/Scotland.
Ich bin groß und schlank.	I am tall and slim.
Ich habe langes, braunes Haar und blaue Augen.	I've got long brown hair and blue eyes.
Wie ist deine Adresse?/Wie ist deine Postleitzahl?	What is your address?/What is your post code?
Ich wohne in der Bahnhofstraße 19. 50739 Köln.	I live at 19 Bahnhofstraße. 50739 Köln.

Meine Familie / My family

Hast du Geschwister?	Have you got brothers and sisters?
Nein, ich bin ein Einzelkind.	No, I am an only child.
Ich habe zwei Brüder und eine Schwester.	I've got two brothers and one sister.
Meine ältere Schwester heißt …	My older sister is called …
Mein jüngerer Bruder ist erst drei Jahre alt.	My younger brother is only three years old.
Wie sieht er/sie aus?	What does he/she look like?
Sie ist klein und ein bisschen dick. Sie trägt eine Brille.	She is small and a bit fat. She wears glasses.
Mein Vater hat einen Schnurrbart./Er ist intelligent und lustig.	My father has a moustache./He is intelligent and funny.
Was macht er gern?	What does he like doing?
Er hört gern Musik und er spielt gern Fußball.	He likes listening to music and he likes playing football.
Meine Schwester liest gern und treibt gern Sport.	My sister likes reading and doing sport.
Hast du Haustiere?	Have you got any pets?
Ich habe einen Hund und ein Meerschweinchen.	I've got a dog and a guinea pig.

Besuch haben / Having visitors

Grüß dich. Willkommen in England!	Hello. Welcome to England!
Komm herein und setz dich.	Come and sit down.
Hier ist meine Mutter.	Here is my mother.
Freut mich.	I'm pleased to meet you.
Hast du eine gute Reise gehabt?	Have you had a good journey?
Ich bin nach der Reise müde.	I am tired after the journey.
Hier ist dein Zimmer.	Here is your bedroom.
Möchtest du etwas essen?	Would you like something to eat?
Vielen Dank für das Essen.	Thank you very much for the meal.

Dein deutscher Freund stellt Fragen über deine Familie.

– Wie sieht deine Schwester aus?
– Sie ist klein und ziemlich schlank.

– Was macht sie gern?
– Sie treibt gern Sport.

– Hast du auch Haustiere?
– Ja, ich habe eine Katze und einen Wellensittich.

1. Practise the dialogue above with your partner until you know it really well.
2. Now write a new dialogue. Change the details in each part to match the following clues:
   - Say your brother is tall and fat; he likes reading and listening to music.
   - Say you have a horse and a rabbit.

Foundation Tier & Foundation/Higher Tier — F&F/H

Exam Practice

A

Read and practise the two role-plays below with your partner.

> *Exam Tip*
> - In your Foundation Tier role-play (the role-play with the smaller number, a number between 1 – 6), each candidate's task can score a maximum of two marks.
> - You get two marks if you complete the task clearly and are easily understood. Remember to pronounce things well.
> - You do not need to answer in detail to score two marks.

Role-play 1

Teacher's Role

Du sprichst mit deinem Freund/deiner Freundin. Ich bin der Freund/die Freundin.
1 Meine Familie ist klein.
2 Ja, ich habe eine Schwester.
3 Das ist schön.
4 Sie ist dreizehn. Wann hast du Geburtstag?
5 Aha.

Candidate's Role

You are talking to your friend about your families.

1 Ask if your friend has any brothers or sisters.
2 Say you have two brothers.
3 Ask how old your friend's sister is.
4 Say when your birthday is.

Your teacher will play the part of your German friend and will speak first.

(Adapted from AQA/NEAB – 1998)

Role-play 2

Teacher's Role

Du bist bei deinem Freund. Der Cousin/die Cousine kommt zu Besuch. Ich bin der Cousin/die Cousine.
1 Guten Tag.
2 Ich bin der Peter/die Petra.
3 In Dortmund.
4 Was machst du gern in deiner Freizeit?
5 Ich auch.

Candidate's Role

You meet your German friend's cousin.

1 Introduce yourself.
2 Ask where the cousin lives.
3 Say where you come from.
4 Say you like playing tennis.

Your teacher will play the part of your friend's cousin and will speak first.

(AQA/NEAB – 1998)

B

> *Exam Tip*
> - In your Foundation/Higher Tier role-play (that is the role-play with the larger number, a number between 7 – 12), each candidate's task can score a maximum of three marks.
> - Again, you get full marks if you complete the task clearly and are easily understood, but with a little more detail. Many tasks will force you to answer in full sentences.

1 Cover the teacher's role and take just four minutes to prepare the candidate's tasks.
2 Uncover the teacher's role. Act out the dialogue with a partner. Then write it out in full and learn it.

Teacher's Role

1 Wie heißt dein Bruder? Wie alt ist er?
2 Wie sieht er aus?
3 Und sonst?
4 Wann und wo hast du ihn zum letzten Mal gesehen?
5 Wir werden ihn bestimmt schnell finden.

Candidate's Role

You are on holiday in Germany. You cannot find your sister. You are talking to the receptionist.
1 Tell him/her your brother's name and age.
2 Describe his eyes and hair.
3 Give two more details about what he looks like.
4 !

Your teacher will play the part of your friend's cousin and will speak first.

(AQA/NEAB – 1998)

Self, Family & Friends

Higher Tier H

Deine Familie | Your family

Meine ältere Schwester ist verheiratet.	My older sister is married.
Sie hat ein Kind.	She has a child.
Meine Eltern sind seit acht Jahren geschieden.	My parents have been divorced for eight years.
Ich komme gut mit meiner Stiefmutter aus.	I get on well with my stepmother.
Wie kommst du mit deinem Bruder aus?	How do you get on with your brother?
Ziemlich gut. Ich finde ihn manchmal ein bisschen dumm, aber er ist erst sechs Jahre alt.	Quite well. I think he's a bit stupid sometimes but he is only six years old.
Kommst du gut mit deiner älteren Schwester aus?	Do you get on well with your older sister?
Manchmal ja, aber nur, wenn sie gut gelaunt ist.	Sometimes I do, but only when she is in a good mood.
Sie ärgert mich, weil sie oft schlecht gelaunt ist.	She annoys me because she is often in a bad mood.
Ich komme nicht so gut mit meinen Eltern aus.	I don't get on so well with my parents.
Sie verstehen mich nicht immer.	They don't always understand me.
Sie sind oft zu streng.	They are often too strict.

Um Erlaubnis bitten | Asking for permission

Darf ich jetzt fernsehen?	May I watch television now?
Darf ich heute Abend in die Disco gehen?	May I go to a disco this evening?
Wann kommst du zurück?	When will you get back?
Ich komme gegen elf Uhr nach Hause.	I'll come home at about eleven o'clock.

Sich entschuldigen | Apologising

Es tut mir wirklich Leid, dass ich nicht geschrieben habe.	I am really sorry that I haven't written.
Ich habe es nicht absichtlich gemacht.	I didn't do it on purpose.

Probleme | Problems

Ich muss am Wochenende schon um zehn Uhr nach Hause kommen.	I have to get home at ten o'clock at the weekend.
Das finde ich nicht richtig.	I don't think that's right.
Was soll ich machen?	What should I do?
Mein Vater versteht sich nie mit meinen Freunden.	My father never gets on with my boyfriends.
Sie behandeln mich wie ein Kind.	They treat me like a child.
Meine Mutter beschwert sich immer, weil ich mein Zimmer nicht aufräume.	My mother always complains because I don't tidy my room.
Ich muss mein Zimmer so oft aufräumen.	I have to tidy my room so often.
Ich darf während der Woche nicht ausgehen.	I'm not allowed to go out during the week.

Du sprichst über deine Familie.

1. Wie ist deine Schwester?
2. Sie ist z … i … aber auch ein b … f …
3. Kommst du gut mit ihr aus?
4. M … j …, besonders, wenn sie g … g … i …
5. Ärgert sie dich auch manchmal?
6. Ja, wenn sie s … g … i …
7. Und wie kommst du mit deinen Eltern aus?
8. Ziemlich g …, aber sie s … oft z … s …
9. Wieso?
10. I … m … am Wochenende immer um halb e … nach Hause k … !

1. Complete the dialogue above.
2. Copy the questions from the dialogue again and write a new answer for each question to describe your family.

Higher Tier H

Exam Practice

H A

1 To prepare for your role-play, you could make "word suns" of phrases to talk about people in your family, as in the one below.

2 Revise the key phrases from pages 26 and 28. Write out as many phrases as possible to describe three other people you know.

3 Now copy and complete the "word sun" below.

H B

1 Cover the teacher's role and the candidate's answers. Take four minutes to prepare the candidate's instructions below. Remember to give detailed answers.

2 Uncover the teacher's role. Check that you have completed all the tasks in your preparation. Write out your completed role-play.

Teacher's Role

1 Hallo! *(Candidate's task: to apologise for not writing and give a reason.)*
2 Wie kommst du mit deiner Schwester aus? *(Candidate's task: to say whether he/she gets on with his/her sister.)*
3 Wie ist deine Schwester? *(Candidate's task: to give two details about his/her sister.)*
4 Ich könnte eine Brieffreundin für deine Schwester finden. Möchte deine Schwester eine Brieffreundin? Warum? Warum nicht? *(Candidate's task: to say whether his/her sister would like a penfriend and why.)*
5 Schon gut.

Candidate's Role

You telephone your German friend to apologise for not writing and he/she asks about your sister.
1 Entschuldigung und Grund
2 Schwester: Verhältnisse
3 Schwester: Charakter
4 !

Your teacher will play the part of your friend and will speak first.

(Adapted from AQA/NEAB)

3 Compare the candidate's answers below with your answer, but add more detail for each answer here to allow the candidate to score more marks.

Candidate's Answers

1 Es tut mir Leid, dass ich nicht geschrieben habe. + ...
   (Candidate should have given a reason.)
2 Ich komme gut mit meiner Schwester aus. + ...
   (Candidate should have given a reason.)
3 Sie ist freundlich. + ...
   (Candidate should have given two details.)
4 Sie möchte gern eine Brieffreundin. + ...
   (Candidate should have given a reason.)

Exam Tip
- To score full marks, make sure you prepare answers which give reasons or more than one detail.

29

Free Time & Special Occasions

Foundation Tier & Foundation/Higher Tier

Meine Freizeit
Was machst du in deiner Freizeit?
Ich sammele Schallplatten.
Ich gehe manchmal ins Hallenbad.
Gehst du gern ins Sportzentrum?
Fährst du oft Rad?
Letztes Wochenende bin ich in den Jugendklub gegangen.
Morgen spiele ich Tischtennis.
Möchtest du mit mir schwimmen gehen?
Was machst du gern?
Ich treibe gern Sport.
Ich gehe nicht gern ins Kino. Ich sehe lieber fern.

My free time
What do you do in your free time?
I collect records.
I sometimes go to the swimming baths.
Do you like going to the sports centre?
Do you often go cycling?
Last weekend, I went to the youth club.
Tomorrow, I'm going to play table tennis.
Would you like to come swimming with me?
What do you like doing?
I like doing sport.
I don't like going to the cinema. I prefer watching television.

Karten kaufen
Was kostet eine Karte?
Zwei Erwachsene und ein Kind.
Ich kaufe die Karten.
Zweimal, bitte.
Ich möchte heute spielen.
Ich möchte eine Stunde spielen.
Wann hat das Hallenbad auf?
Ich mag die Musik

Buying tickets
How much does a ticket cost?
Two adults and a child.
I'll buy the tickets.
Two, please.
I'd like to play today.
I'd like to play for one hour.
When are the swimming baths open?
I like the music.

Taschengeld
Bekommst du Taschengeld?
Wie viel Taschengeld bekommst du?
Ich bekomme kein Taschengeld.
Was für Arbeit machst du, um Geld zu verdienen?
Ich arbeite in einem Café, um Geld zu verdienen.
Ich bekomme fünf Pfund pro Woche.
Meine Eltern geben mir Geld.
Was machst du mit dem Geld?
Ich kaufe Kleidung und Zeitschriften.
Ich spare mein Geld.

Pocket money
Do you get pocket money?
How much pocket money do you get?
I don't get any pocket money.
What sort of work do you do to earn money?
I work in a café to earn money.
I get five pounds a week.
My parents give me money.
What do you do with the money?
I buy clothes and magazines.
I save my money.

Du sprichst über deine Hobbys.

1. Work with a partner and practise reading the dialogue aloud.
2. Write a new dialogue for the cartoon by changing the underlined words.
3. Change the underlined words in the cartoon again and answer each question to describe your interests.

Exam Practice

A

1 Cover the model dialogues and prepare the candidate's tasks. Uncover the model dialogue, write out the role-plays in full and practise them with a partner.

Role-play 1

Candidate's Role

You are in Germany and want to play tennis. You and your friend go to a club to make enquiries.
1 Say you would like to play tennis today.
2 Ask what time you can play.
3 Ask what it costs.
4 Say you want to play for an hour.

Your teacher will play the part of the tennis-court attendant and will speak first.

Model Dialogue

Du willst Tennis spielen. Ich bin der/die Angestellte.
1 Guten Morgen. Bitte schön?
   I ... m ... h ... T ... s ...
2 Ja, natürlich.
   W ... k ... w ... s ... ?
3 Um elf Uhr.
   W ... k ... e .., b .. ?
4 DM 6,00.
   W ... m ... e ... S ... s ...

(AQA/NEAB – 1997)

Exam Tip

- Read your tasks carefully. If you are told to say you like something, use *ich mag* or *gern* + a verb, e.g.:
  Say you like dancing. *Ich tanze gern.*
  Say you like the music. *Ich mag die Musik.*

- If you are told to say you would like something, use *möchte*, e.g.
  Say you would like to go swimming.
  Ich möchte schwimmen gehen.

Role-play 2

Candidate's Role

You are talking about hobbies with your German friend.

1 Say you like doing sport.
2 Ask your friend what his/her hobbies are.
3 Ask if your friend would like to go cycling with you.
4 Say you are going at 11 o'clock.

Your teacher will play the part of your friend and will speak first.

Model Dialogue

Dein deutscher Freund/deine deutsche Freundin ist bei dir zu Besuch. Ich bin der Freund/die Freundin.
1 Was machen wir am Wochenende?
   I ... t ... S ... g ...
2 Das gefällt mir nicht.
   W ... m ... d ... g ... ?
3 Ich wandere gern.
   M ... d ... m ... m ... R ... f ... ?
4 Ja, gern. Wann gehen wir?
   I ... g ... u ... e ... U ...
5 Schön, ich freue mich darauf!

(Adapted from AQA/NEAB – 1998)

B

1 Cover the teacher's role and take just four minutes to prepare the candidate's tasks. Then uncover the teacher's role and act out the dialogue with a partner.

Teacher's Role

1 Wie viel Taschengeld bekommst du?
2 Was machst du mit dem Geld?
3 Ich auch.
4 Ich arbeite nicht. Was machst du, um Geld zu verdienen?
5 Das ist gut.

Candidate's Role

You are talking to your Austrian friend about pocket money and jobs.
1 Tell him/her how much pocket money you get and how often.
2 Tell him/her what you do with the money.
3 Ask what kind of job your friend has.
4 !

Your teacher will play the part of your friend and will speak first.

(AQA/NEAB – 1997)

Free Time & Special Occasions

Higher Tier H

Was ich gern und nicht gern mache

Am liebsten spiele ich Tennis, weil ich gut spielen kann.

Fußball gefällt mir nicht, weil es so langweilig ist.
Ich schwimme sehr gern, aber nur im Freibad, wenn das Wetter warm ist.
Ich schwimme lieber im Hallenbad als im Meer.
Das Meer ist mir immer zu kalt.
Wir könnten am Samstag dorthin gehen.
Ich bin Mitglied eines Fußballvereins.
Am Wochenende gehe ich zu jedem Spiel.
Letzte Woche haben wir gegen eine Mannschaft aus Birmingham gespielt.
Wir haben gewonnen/verloren.

Die Freizeit

Hast du heute etwas vor?
Was möchtest du morgen Abend machen?
Was schlägst du vor?
Ich möchte zu diesem Konzert gehen.
Letzten Samstag war ich bei einem Rugbyspiel.
Die Mannschaft hat sehr gut gespielt.
Gehen wir morgen einkaufen?
Wenn es regnet, bleibe ich lieber zu Hause.

Ausflüge

Wie lange dauert der Ausflug?
An welchem Tag ist der Ausflug?
Wann fährt der Bus ab?
Wann sind wir zurück?
Wir können unterwegs essen.
Sie übernachten in einem Hotel.
Sie essen zu Mittag in einem Restaurant.
Sie müssen Lunchpakete mitnehmen.

What I like and don't like doing

The thing I like doing best is playing tennis because I can play well.
I don't like football because it is so boring.
I like swimming but only in an open-air pool when the weather is warm.
I'd rather swim in the swimming baths than in the sea.
The sea is always too cold for me.
We could go there on Saturday.
I am a member of a football club.
At the weekend, I go to every game.
Last week, we played against a team from Birmingham.

We won/lost.

Free time

Have you got any plans for today?
What would you like to do tomorrow evening?
What do you suggest?
I'd like to go to this concert.
Last Saturday, I went to a rugby match.
The team played very well.
Shall we go shopping tomorrow?
If it rains, I'd prefer to stay at home.

Excursions

How long does the excursion last?
On which day is the excursion?
When does the bus leave?
When do we get back?
We can eat during the journey.
You stay the night in a hotel.
You have lunch in a restaurant.
You must take packed lunches with you.

Du sprichst mit deiner Freundin.

1. Practise the dialogue above with your partner.
2. Cover the dialogue. Now look at these cue words for the candidate's role and write the whole dialogue from memory.

Candidate's Role
- diese Woche
- Ausflug
- Tage
- Wie lange?
- Übernachtung
- Essen

32

Higher Tier H

Exam Practice

1 Revise pages 30 and 32 and make sure you know all the phrases. Cover the teacher's role and the model dialogue. Give yourself just four minutes to prepare the candidate's role.

Candidate's Role

You are staying with a family in Germany and are discussing plans for an outing. You are keen to go walking and want to persuade your hosts to go on one of the walking tours described in this brochure.

1 *Wanderung*
2 *Warum?*
3 *!*
4 *Wanderrouten*

Your teacher will play the part of your friend and will speak first.

Wandern ohne Gepäck
Wir haben 10 wunderschöne Wanderrouten, zum Beispiel:

Route 5: 2-Tage Wanderung ohne Gepäck durch den Schwarzwald

2 Übernachtungen im Doppelzimmer mit Dusche und WC
2 x Frühstück, 1 x Mittagessen.

Unser Preis: NUR DM 153,- pro Person

Weitere Informationen und Reservierungen:

Wandern Ohne Gepäck
Postfach 11 45
58011 HAGEN

Tel: 02331 / 68 09 74

---

2 Now look at the teacher's role. Work with a partner and help each other to make up the best answers. Remember either to give more than one detail in each answer or be prepared to give a reason for your answer. You will need to do this to score your four marks per answer.

Teacher's Role

1 Mein Vater hat nur drei Tage Urlaub. Genügt das, eine Wanderung zu machen? *(Candidate's task: to say how long the walk lasts.)*
2 Ich finde lange Wanderungen mit schwerem Rucksack sehr anstrengend. *(Candidate's task: to counter suggestions that it is too tiring.)*
3 Und wie ist es mit dem Essen? *(Candidate's task: to explain what meals are provided.)*
4 Ich kenne den Schwarzwald sehr gut. Gibt es noch andere Wanderungen? *(Candidate's task: to say there are other routes.)*
5 Schön. Ich werde mal anrufen.

(Adapted from AQA/NEAB – 1997)

3 Read the model dialogue and compare it with your answer. Notice how the candidate gives all the necessary information in each answer. The teacher does not have to ask additional questions to allow the candidate to complete the tasks.
4 Write out your completed role-play and learn it.

Model Dialogue

– *Mein Vater hat nur drei Tage Urlaub. Genügt das, eine Wanderung zu machen?*
– **Wir haben Zeit. Die Wanderung dauert nur zwei Tage.**
– *Ich finde lange Wanderungen mit schwerem Rucksack sehr anstrengend.*
– **Du musst keinen Rucksack tragen. Das Gepäck kommt mit dem Bus.**
– *Und wie ist es mit dem Essen?*
– **Wir frühstücken im Hotel und bekommen mittags ein Lunchpacket.**
– *Ich kenne den Schwarzwald sehr gut. Gibt es noch andere Wanderungen?*
– **Ja, es gibt zehn wunderschöne Wanderrouten. Wir könnten in den Bergen wandern.**
– *Schön. Ich werde mal anrufen.*

Leisure & Arranging a Meeting

Foundation Tier & Foundation/Higher Tier — F&F/H

Vorschläge und Einladungen	**Suggestions and invitations**
Was machen wir heute?	What shall we do today?
Möchtest du heute Abend ins Kino gehen?	Would you like to go to the cinema this evening?
Gehen wir spazieren?	Shall we go for a walk?
Das möchte ich gern.	I'd like that.
Leider kann ich nicht zum Spiel kommen.	Unfortunately, I can't come to the match.
Wann und wo treffen wir uns?	When and where shall we meet?
Treffen wir uns um vier Uhr?	Shall we meet at four o'clock?
Treffen wir uns an der Bushaltestelle?/Bei mir?	Shall we meet at the bus stop?/At my house?
Bis acht Uhr. Tschüs!	See you at eight o'clock. Good bye.
Karten kaufen	**Buying tickets**
Gibt es eine Ermäßigung für Studenten?	Is there a reduction for students?
Zweimal, bitte.	Two tickets, please.
Für welche Vorstellung möchten Sie Karten?	For which performance would you like tickets?
Für welchen Tag?	For which day?
Wie lange dauert die Vorstellung?	How long does the performance last?
Wann beginnt das Konzert?	When does the concert begin?
Wann ist das Spiel zu Ende?	When does the match end?
Was läuft?	**What's on?**
Was läuft heute im Kino?	What's on at the cinema today?
Was für ein Film ist es?	What sort of film is it?
Es ist eine Komödie/ein Krimi.	It is a comedy/a thriller.
Wie hat dir der Film gefallen?	How did you like the film?
Das Konzert war toll.	The concert was great.
Freizeit	**Free time**
Was gibt es heute Abend im Fernsehen?	What's on television this evening?
Es gibt eine Sendung über Pferde.	There is a programme about horses.
Darf ich bitte fernsehen?	May I please watch television?
Kann ich bitte meine Eltern anrufen?	Can I please phone my parents?
Ich habe einen sehr guten Film gesehen.	I saw a very good film.
Der Film war doof/schlecht, oder?	The film was stupid/bad, wasn't it?
Ich lese sehr gern Zeitschriften.	I like reading magazines.

Du machst Pläne für einen Kinobesuch.

1. In this dialogue, only the top half of all the words is printed. Re-write the dialogue in full.
2. Practise the dialogue with your partner, taking it in turns to ask and answer the questions.
3. Write a new dialogue by changing one detail in each answer, e.g. *Gehen wir ins Konzert?*

Foundation Tier &
Foundation/Higher Tier **F&F/H**

Exam Practice

 A

Use the pictures below to make as many different dialogues as possible.

Example

A: Was möchtest du machen?   B: Gehen wir ins Kino?
A: Wann treffen wir uns?   B: Um acht Uhr.
A: Wo treffen wir uns?   B: In der Stadt.
A: Bis acht Uhr. Tschüs!   B: Tschüs!

a Was möchtest du machen?

b Wann treffen wir uns?

c Wo treffen wir uns?

F B

Read the candidate's instructions for these two role-plays. Then read the candidate's answers.
They are all in the wrong order. Select the correct answers to complete the candidate's tasks.

Candidate's Role	**Candidate's Role**	**Model Answers**
You go to a concert in Germany with a friend. 1 Ask what the tickets cost. 2 Ask for two tickets. 3 Ask what time the concert begins. 4 Say you like the group. (AQA/NEAB – 1998)	You have had a meal with a German family. They invite you to go to the cinema tomorrow. 1 Ask when you are going. 2 Ask where you are going to meet. 3 Say the meal was good. 4 Thank your host and say good bye. (Adapted from AQA/NEAB – 1997)	a Das Essen war lecker. b Zweimal, bitte. c Wo treffen wir uns? d Ich mag die Gruppe. e Was kostet eine Karte? f Wann beginnt das Konzert? g Wann gehen wir ins Kino? h Vielen Dank. Auf Wiedersehen.

C

1 Cover the teacher's role below and work with a partner. Take turns to plan what each of you will say as the candidate. (Time each other so that you know how long it has taken you to prepare. Remember that you will only have four minutes in your exam. If you are taking too long, go back to page 34 and learn your phrases again. The better you know your phrases the less time you will need to prepare your role-play.)
2 Now look at the teacher's role and practise the whole role-play with your partner.
3 Write out the role-play in full and learn it.

Teacher's Role	**Candidate's Role**
1 Guten Abend. Wie viele sind Sie, bitte? 2 Ja, gut. 3 Ja, 30 Prozent. Für welche Vorstellung und für welchen Tag möchten Sie die Karten? 4 Kein Problem. 5 Zwei Stunden.	You are in a German theatre buying tickets. 1 Tell him/her there is one adult and two students. 2 Ask if there is a reduction for students. 3 ! 4 Ask how long the play lasts. Your teacher will play the part of the cashier and will speak first.

(Adapted from AQA/NEAB – 1998)

Leisure & Arranging a Meeting

Higher Tier H

Freizeit	**Free time**
Kann man hier Tennis spielen?	Can you play tennis here?
Gibt es ein Theater in der Stadt?	Is there a theatre in town?
Wir könnten vielleicht ins Theater gehen.	We could perhaps go to the theatre.
Das wäre schön.	That would be nice.
Ich freue mich darauf.	I'm looking forward to that.
Ich möchte lieber zu Hause bleiben.	I'd rather stay at home.
Ich möchte dich lieber bei mir treffen.	I'd rather meet you at my house.
Sollen wir um neun Uhr losfahren?	Should we set off at nine o'clock?
Abgemacht.	Agreed.
Leider kann ich nicht vor neunzehn Uhr kommen, weil ich arbeiten muss.	Unfortunately, I can't come before nine o'clock because I have to work.

Vorschläge	**Suggestions**
Sehen wir mal in der Zeitung nach?	Shall we look in the newspaper?
Wir könnten das Kino anrufen.	We could phone the cinema.
Es ist ein großes Abenteuer/eine Liebesgeschichte.	It is an adventure/a love story.
Wovon handelt der Film?	What is the film about?
Der Film hat mir sehr gut/gar nicht gut gefallen.	I liked the film very much/not at all.
Er war sehr spannend/komisch.	It was very exciting/funny.

Lesen und Fernsehen	**Reading and television**
Was liest du gern?	What do you like reading?
Ich lese nicht viel.	I don't read much.
Wenn ich lese, lese ich lieber Zeitschriften.	When I read I prefer to read magazines.
Hast du die Nachrichten im Fernsehen gesehen?	Have you seen the news on television?
Was für Sendungen siehst du gern?	What sort of programmes do you like?
Ich sehe gern Sportsendungen.	I like watching sports programmes.
Ich sehe dreimal in der Woche eine Fernsehserie.	I watch a serial three times a week.
Es handelt sich um Familien, die alle in derselben Straße wohnen.	It is about families who all live in the same street.
Sie spielt in den Bergen.	It takes place in the mountains.

Du sprichst mit deiner deutschen Freundin über Filme.

1. Read the dialogue in this cartoon.
2. Re-write the dialogue to describe a film of your choice. Write three sentences to say what the film is about and why you like it. Finally, suggest another activity which you could do while the film is being recorded on video.

36

Higher Tier H

Exam Practice

1 In the two role-plays below, prepare what you are going to say without looking at the teacher's role.
2 Then look at the teacher's role and practise the whole role-play with your partner.
3 Finally, look at the model dialogue for Role-play 1 and adapt your role-play if necessary.
4 Write out both these role-plays and learn them.

Exam Tip
- In this role-play, you have to describe briefly what happens in a film. This is something you need to prepare and learn before your exam. Choose a film and prepare two simple sentences to describe what happens. Be ready also to say what you think of the film and why.
- You may have to describe your favourite television programme in the same way.

Role-play 1

Teacher's Role

1 Was ist dein Lieblingsfilm? *(Candidate's task: to say which film he/she has enjoyed.)*
2 Warum? *(Candidate's task: to say why he/she likes that film.)*
3 Wovon handelt der Film? *(Candidate's task: to give two details of the story.)*
4 Möchtest du jetzt einen deutschen Film sehen? *(Candidate's task: to accept or decline the invitation and say why.)*
5 Abgemacht!

Candidate's Role

You and your German friend are talking about films. Your friend is very interested in films. You like films, but you are more interested in sport.
1 *Lieblingsfilm*
2 *Warum?*
3 *!*
4 *Einladung*

Your teacher will play the part of your friend and will speak first.

Model Dialogue

– *Was ist dein Lieblingsfilm?*
– **Titanic hat mir gut gefallen.**
– *Warum?*
– **Die Schauspieler waren sehr gut und die Spezialeffekte waren super.**
– *Wovon handelt der Film?*
– **Es handelt sich um das Schiff Titanic, das gesunken ist, aber es ist auch eine Liebesgeschichte zwischen einer jungen, reichen Dame und einem armen Künstler. Die Dame wird gerettet und der Künstler ertrinkt. Es ist sehr traurig.**
– *Möchtest du jetzt einen deutschen Film sehen?*
– **Ich möchte lieber ins Sportzentrum gehen. Ich gehe nicht so gern ins Kino.**
– *Abgemacht!*

Role-play 2

Exam Tip
- In this role-play, you have to negotiate. Always be prepared to suggest an alternative activity or another time and place.

Teacher's Role

1 Ich freue mich darauf, heute Nachmittag ins Museum zu gehen. *(Candidate's task: to say that he/she doesn't like museums.)*
2 Echt! Was möchtest du denn lieber machen? *(Candidate's task: to respond with an alternative suggestion.)*
3 Das gefällt mir nicht. Was können wir sonst noch machen? *(Candidate's task: to suggest an alternative activity.)*
4 Gute Idee! Wann und wo machen wir das? *(Candidate's task: to finalise arrangements.)*
5 Abgemacht! Ich freue mich darauf.

Candidate's Role

You are staying with your friend in Germany. Your friend has arranged a visit to a local museum, but you prefer to be out in the open air.
1 *deine Meinung*
2 *deine Alternative*
3 *!*
4 *Verabredung – wann und wo*

Your teacher will play the part of your friend and will speak first.

37

Home Town & Customs

Foundation Tier & Foundation/Higher Tier

Deine Stadt und deine Gegend
Ich wohne in einer großen/kleinen Stadt im Norden/Süden/Osten/Westen von England/Schottland/Irland/Wales.
Was für eine Stadt ist es?
Die Stadt ist alt und ziemlich schön.
Es ist eine Industriestadt/Touristenstadt.
Was gibt es in der Stadt?
Es gibt ein altes Rathaus und einen berühmten Dom.
Was kann man in der Stadt machen?
Man kann Sport treiben.
Die Gegend ist herrlich.
Es gibt schöne Hügel und Wälder.
Man kann am Strand spazieren gehen.
Wie gefällt dir die Stadt?
Ich wohne sehr gern hier. Es gibt viel für junge Leute.
Mir gefällt die Stadt nicht.
Es ist langweilig. Es gibt nichts zu tun.

Your town and your region
I live in a large/small town in the north/south/east/west of England/Scotland/Ireland/Wales.
What sort of town is it?
The town is old and quite nice.
It is an industrial/tourist town.
What is there in the town?
There is an old town hall and a famous cathedral.
What is there to do in the town?
You can do sport.
The surrounding area is wonderful.
There are lovely hills and woods.
You can go for walks on the beach.
How do you like the town?
I like living here. There is a lot for young people.
I don't like the town.
It is boring. There is nothing to do.

Besuch in der Stadt
Was gibt es in der Stadt zu sehen?
Dort drüben ist der Marktplatz.
Wie fährt man in die Stadt?
Man kann mit dem Bus in die Stadt fahren.
Wie oft fährt der Bus?
Alle zehn Minuten.
Wie lange dauert die Fahrt?
Die Fahrt dauert eine Viertelstunde.

Visiting a town
What is there to see in town?
The market place is over there.
How do you get into town?
You can go into town by bus.
How often does the bus go?
Every ten minutes.
How long does the journey last?
The journey lasts a quarter of an hour.

Feste
Was machst du zu Weihnachten?
Ich besuche meine Großeltern.
Ich kaufe Geschenke und Karten.
Am Heiligabend gehen wir in die Kirche.
Zu Silvester gehe ich in die Disco.
Zum Geburtstag bekomme ich Geschenke.
Was möchtest du zu deinem nächsten Geburtstag machen?

Festivals
What do you do at Christmas?
I visit my grandparents.
I buy presents and cards.
On Christmas Eve, we go to church.
On New's Year Eve, I go to a disco.
On my birthday, I get presents.
What would you like to do on your next birthday?

Das Wetter
Im Winter schneit es oft.
Im Herbst ist es manchmal nebelig.
Im Sommer gibt es manchmal Gewitter.
Es donnert und blitzt.
In dieser Gegend ist es sehr windig. Gestern hat es stark geregnet.

The weather
It often snows in winter.
It is sometimes foggy in autumn.
There are sometimes storms in summer.
It thunders and there is lightning.
In this area, it is very windy. Yesterday, it rained hard.

Du beantwortest Fragen über deine Stadt und über deine Gegend.

Wo wohnst du? — Ichwohneineinerstadtinnordengland.

Was für eine Stadt ist es? — Esisteinegroßeindustriestadt.

Was gibt es in der Stadt? — Esgibtvielegeschäfteundzweidiscos.

1. Correct the boy's answers above and write out the whole dialogue.
2. Practise with a partner, taking turns to ask and answer the questions.
3. Now write a new dialogue with your own answers to these questions.

Foundation Tier &
Foundation/Higher Tier F&F/H

Exam Practice

F A

Use the illustrations to complete the two dialogues below.

Dialogue 1

Was gibt es in deiner Stadt?

Wie kommt man in die Stadt?

Was kann man in der Gegend machen?

Dialogue 2

Wo wohnst du?

Was für ein Dorf ist es?

Wie ist das Wetter im Sommer?

F B

Practise this role-play with your partner. Write out the complete role-play and learn it.

Teacher's Role	Candidate's Role
Du sprichst mit deinem deutschen Freund/deiner deutschen Freundin. Ich bin der Freund/die Freundin. 1 Wo wohnst du? 2 Was für eine Stadt ist es? 3 Ich wohne auch in einer modernen kleinen Stadt. 4 Nicht sehr viel. Es ist langweilig und das Wetter ist nicht gut. Wie ist das Wetter in deiner Stadt? 5 Hier auch.	You are talking with your German friend about where you live. 1 Say you live in the North of England. 2 Say it is a small modern town. 3 Ask your friend what there is to do in his/her town. 4 Say it often rains. Your teacher will play the part of your friend and will speak first.

C

1 Cover the teacher's role and write a list of possible questions which your teacher might ask you for the ! task. Compare your list with your partner's. Decide on two questions which your teacher is most likely to ask. Prepare an answer for each.
2 Uncover the teacher's role. Did you predict the ! question correctly? Practise the whole role-play with your partner.
3 Write out the completed role-play and learn it.

Teacher's Role	Candidate's Role
1 Wann hast du Geburtstag? 2 Was passiert an dem Tag? 3 Was machst du normalerweise? 4 Was möchtest du an deinem Geburtstag machen? 5 Schön.	You are talking with your Austrian friend about birthdays. 1 Tell him/her when your birthday is. 2 Tell him/her you get presents and cards. 3 Tell him/her you stay at home. 4 ! Your teacher will play the part of your friend and will speak first.

39

Home Town & Customs

Higher Tier H

Deine Stadt und deine Gegend
Im Winter ist es in Österreich kälter als bei uns.
Bei uns gibt es nicht viel Schnee.
Man kann in Österreich besser Ski laufen.
In der Schweiz gibt es hohe Berge.
Es ist dort viel ruhiger.
Ich wohne gern hier, weil es viel für junge Leute gibt.
Ich wohne nicht gern hier, weil es viel Industrie gibt.
Ich möchte lieber in den USA wohnen.
Es ist modern und man kann dort so viel machen.
Ich würde lieber an der Küste wohnen, weil ich gern segle.
Ich würde lieber auf dem Land wohnen, weil es nicht so laut ist.
Ich würde lieber in einer kleinen Stadt wohnen,
weil es hier zu viele Touristen gibt.

Your town and your region
It's colder in Austria in winter than it is here.
We don't get a lot of snow.
You can ski better in Austria.
In Switzerland, there are high mountains.
It is much quieter there.
I like living here because there is a lot for young people.
I don't like living here because there is a lot of industry.
I would prefer to live in the U.S.A.
It is modern and you can do so much there.
I would prefer to live at the coast because I like sailing.
I would prefer to live in the country because it is not so noisy.
I would prefer to live in a small town
because there are too many tourists here.

Feste
Was ist das wichtigste Fest für deine Familie?
Mein Geburtstag ist mein Lieblingsfest, weil ich mit meinen Freunden ausgehen kann.
Zu Weihnachten essen wir Pute mit Gemüse.

Festivals
What is the most important festival for your family?
My birthday is my favourite festival because
I can go out with my friends.
At Christmas, we eat turkey with vegetables.

Das Wetter
Wie wird das Wetter morgen sein?
Wie ist die Wettervorhersage?
Am Vormittag wird die Sonne scheinen. Morgen wird es regnen.
Es wird kalt sein.
Am Nachmittag wird es schneien.

The weather
What is the weather going to be like tomorrow?
What is the weather forecast?
In the morning, the sun is going to shine. Tomorrow, it's going to rain.
It is going to be cold.
In the afternoon, it is going to snow.

Du beschreibst deine Stadt.

A
- Wie gefällt dir deine Stadt?
- Ich wohne nicht besonders gern hier.
- Warum?
- Weil es zu viele Touristen gibt.
- Wo würdest du lieber wohnen?
- Ich würde lieber auf dem Land wohnen, weil es ruhiger ist.

Du machst Pläne für morgen und möchtest wissen, wie das Wetter sein wird.

B
- Wie wird das Wetter morgen sein?
- Ich weiß nicht. Sehen wir uns mal die Wettervorhersage in der Zeitung an.
- Was steht dort?
- Morgen Vormittag wird es heiß und sonnig sein.
- Und am Nachmittag? Wie wird es am Nachmittag sein?
- Es wird Gewitter geben. Es wird donnern und blitzen.

1. Practise reading each dialogue aloud with your partner.
2. Partner A covers the cartoon and partner B plays the part of the boy and asks the questions.

40

Higher Tier H

Exam Practice

H A
Here is a list of the sort of questions your teacher could ask on this topic. Answer each question. You must give at least one reason for each answer.
1. Warum wohnst du gern hier?
2. Warum gefällt dir diese Gegend nicht?
3. Warum gefällt dir diese Stadt nicht?
4. Möchtest du lieber in Deutschland oder in England wohnen? Warum?
5. Was ist dein Lieblingsfest? Warum?

H B
1. Cover the teacher's role and the candidate's answers in the role-play below. Read and prepare the candidate's role. Be ready to give more than one detail in each answer or to give a reason for your answer.

Teacher's Role
1. Also, wie gefällt dir mein Dorf? *(Candidate's task: to say whether he/she likes the village and why.)*
2. Würdest du lieber hier wohnen als in England? *(Candidate's task: to say where he/she would rather live and why.)*
3. Wie ist deine Stadt in England? *(Candidate's task: to describe where he/she lives – two details needed.)*
4. Was sind die Unterschiede zwischen deiner Stadt und meinem Dorf hier? *(Candidate's task: to compare the two places – two details needed.)*
5. Das stimmt.

Candidate's Role
You are staying in a village in Switzerland. You and your Swiss friend are talking about the village.
1. deine Meinung
2. !
3. deine Stadt
4. Unterschiede

Your teacher will play the part of your friend and will speak first.

2. Now read the teacher's role and the candidate's answer. Each answer in the Higher Tier role-play carries a maximum of four marks. Look at the marks the candidate scored. Explain why he/she lost marks. Re-write each answer to score the full four marks.
3. Practise the role-play with your partner.

Candidate's Answers
– Also, wie gefällt dir mein Dorf?
– **Es gefällt mir gut.** (2 marks)
– Würdest du lieber hier wohnen als in England?
– **In England.** (0 marks)
– Wie ist deine Stadt in England?
– **Sie ist klein.** (1 mark)
– Was sind die Unterschiede zwischen deiner Stadt und meinem Dorf hier?
– **Meine Stadt ist größer.** (2 marks)
– Das stimmt.

H C
Imagine that you are staying in the Austrian village in this picture. Write a new dialogue in which you compare your home town, village or city with this Austrian village.

Finding the Way

Foundation Tier & Foundation/Higher Tier F&F/H

Fragen, wo es ist
Wo ist die Bushaltestelle?
Wo ist hier ein Parkplatz?
Wie komme ich zur Autobahn?
Wie komme ich zum Flughafen?
Gibt es hier einen Bahnhof?
Wo ist die nächste Tankstelle?
Gibt es in der Nähe eine Bäckerei?

Asking where something is
Where is the bus stop?
Where is there a car park here?
How do I get to the motorway?
How do I get to the airport?
Is there a station here?
Where is the next petrol station?
Is there a baker's nearby?

Sagen, wo es ist
Sie gehen rechts/links/geradeaus.
Sie nehmen die erste Straße rechts.
Sie nehmen die zweite/dritte Straße links.
An der Post gehen Sie links.
Sie gehen über die Brücke.
Sie gehen am Supermarkt vorbei.
Sie gehen bis zum Dom.
Das Rathaus ist gegenüber dem Bahnhof.
Die Kirche ist am Marktplatz.
Das Restaurant ist neben dem Kino.

Saying where something is
You go right/left/straight on.
You take the first street on the right.
You take the second/third street on the left.
At the post office, you turn left.
You go over the bridge.
You go past the supermarket.
You go up to the cathedral.
The town hall is opposite the station.
The church is on the market place.
The restaurant is next to the cinema.

Wie weit ist es?
Ist es weit?
Wie weit ist es?
Es ist hier in der Nähe.
Es ist nur fünf Minuten zu Fuß von hier.
Ungefähr drei Kilometer.
Wie komme ich am besten dahin?
Am besten fahren Sie mit dem Bus.
Vielen Dank.
Auf Wiedersehen.

How far is it?
Is it far?
How far is it?
It is near here.
It is only five minutes on foot from here.
Approximately three kilometres.
What's the best way of getting there?
It's best to take the bus.
Thank you very much.
Good bye.

Du bist in der Stadt und möchtest Briefmarken kaufen.

A: W ... k ... i ... z ... P ..., b ...?
— Du gehst hier geradeaus.
— Hier geradeaus.
— Ja, dann nimmst du die zweite Straße rechts.
— I ... e ... w ... ?
— Nein, es ist nur zwei Minuten von hier.

Du möchtest zum Bahnhof gehen.

B: — Weit?

1. Complete the dialogues in the two cartoons and practise them with your partner.
2. Make up two more dialogues with your partner by changing some details in dialogue **B**, e.g. *Wie komme ich zur Bushaltestelle?*

Foundation Tier & Foundation/Higher Tier F&F/H

Exam Practice

> *Exam Tip*
> - Remember that you will always have to ask at least one question in your Foundation Tier role-play.
> - In your role-plays, the topic of "Finding the Way" will usually be combined with another topic. It is important to practise combining topics in this way. Before you do the tasks below, revise the following topics: Free Time & Special Occasions (page 30); Leisure & Arranging a Meeting (page 34); Home Town & Customs (page 40).

F A

Cover the previous page. Without looking at the key phrases for other topics, write the German for each task below.

a Ask how to get to the station.
b Say you take the third on the right.
c Ask where the nearest restaurant is.
d Say it is raining.
e Ask if it is far.
f Say it's best to go by bus.
g Ask when you are going to the cinema.
h Say you are going to the theatre tomorrow.
i Say it's about fifteen minutes from here.
j Say the theatre is opposite the museum.

F B

1 Work with a partner and complete the role-play below. Then write out the role-play in full.
2 With a partner, change one detail in the role-play. Act out your new role-play. Can the rest of the class spot where you have changed the role-play?

Teacher's Role	**Candidate's Role**
Du bist auf Urlaub bei einer deutschen Familie. Ich bin dein Freund/deine Freundin. 1 Gehen wir aus? 2 Wohin gehen wir? 3 Gute Idee! 4 Ungefähr zwei Kilometer. 5 Um 10 Uhr.	You are staying with your German friend and are planning an outing. 1 Say it's nice weather. 2 Say you would like to go to the castle. 3 Ask how far away it is. 4 Ask when you are going. Your teacher will play the part of your friend and will speak first.

(AQA/NEAB – 1998)

F/H C

1 In the role-play below, cover the teacher's role. Try to predict the questions you may be asked when you see **!** and prepare answers to these questions.
2 Uncover the teacher's role and complete the role-play.

Teacher's Role	**Candidate's Role**
	You are planning the day with your German friend.
1 Ach, es regnet wieder! 2 Wir könnten ins Museum gehen. 3 Ungefähr zehn Minuten. 4 Kein Problem. Was möchtest du heute Abend machen? 5 Gute Idee!	1 Ask your friend what you are going to do today. 2 Ask how far it is. 3 Tell him/her you would like to go by bus. 4 **!**

43

On the Road

Higher Tier H

Die richtige Straße finden
Wie komme ich am besten zur Stadtmitte?
Sie fahren bis zur Ampel.
An der Ampel fahren Sie links.
An der Kreuzung fahren Sie rechts.
Sie verlassen die Autobahn an der nächsten Ausfahrt.
Es gibt ein Parkhaus in der Stadt.

An der Tankstelle
Volltanken, bitte. Zwanzig Liter Normal/Super/Bleifrei.
Können Sie bitte das Öl/die Reifen/das Wasser prüfen?
Verkaufen Sie Straßenkarten?
Nummer drei. Was macht das, bitte?

Eine Panne haben
Ich habe eine Panne. Ich habe eine Reifenpanne.
Könnten Sie einen Mechaniker schicken?
Was ist los? Wo liegt das Problem genau?
Die Bremsen funktionieren nicht richtig.
Der Motor funktioniert nicht.
Es gibt ein komisches Geräusch im Motor.
Wo sind Sie genau?
Ich bin auf der Bundesstraße/Autobahn zwischen Bonn und Köln.
Ich bin zehn Kilometer von Bonn entfernt.
Ich bin ganz in der Nähe von Heilbronn.
Es ist ein weißer VW. Das Kennzeichen ist L364 RUF.
Wir sind in einer halben Stunde da.
Ich warte in meinem Auto.
Können Sie es heute reparieren?
Ich brauche das Auto morgen früh.
Die Fähre fährt um zwanzig Uhr.
Wie lange wird es dauern?

Finding the right road
What is the best way to the town centre?
You go up to the traffic lights.
At the traffic lights, turn left.
At the cross roads, turn right.
You leave the motorway at the next exit.
There is a multi-storey car park in town.

At the petrol station
Fill it up, please. Twenty litres of 3 star/4 star/lead-free petrol.
Can you check the oil/the tyres/the water, please?
Do you sell maps?
(Pump) Number three. How much is that, please?

Breaking down
I've broken down. I've got a flat tyre.
Could you send a mechanic?
What is wrong? What exactly is wrong?
The brakes are not working properly.
There is something wrong with the engine.
There is a funny noise in the engine.
Where are you exactly?
I am on the main road/motorway between Bonn and Cologne.
I am ten kilometres away from Bonn.
I am very close to Heilbronn.
It is a white VW. The registration is L364 RUF.
We'll be there in half an hour.
I'll wait in my car.
Can you repair it today?
I need the car tomorrow morning.
The ferry goes at 8 p.m.
How long will it take?

Du bist mit Freunden in Deutschland im Auto unterwegs. Plötzlich funktionieren die Bremsen nicht richtig. Du rufst eine Reparaturwerkstatt an.

Panel 1: Reparaturwerkstatt Schmidt. Wie kann ich Ihnen helfen? — I ... h ... e ... P ...
Panel 2: Was ist los? — D ... B ... f ... n ... r ...
Panel 3: Wo sind Sie genau? — I ... b ... a ... d ... A ... z ... Köln und Leverkusen.
Panel 4: Ich schicke einen Mechaniker. Wo werden Sie warten? — I ... w ... i ... A ...
Panel 5: W ... l ... w ... e ... d ... ? — Ich weiß nicht genau.
Panel 6: I ... b ... h ... A ... d ... A ... — Kein Problem.

1. Work with a partner and complete the dialogue above. Take it in turns to play the part of the motorist.
2. Write a new dialogue based on the following instructions:
   - There is a strange noise in your engine.
   - You are on a main road between Mannheim and Heidelberg.
   - You decide to wait for the mechanic in a restaurant opposite your car.
   - You need to travel tomorrow morning.

Higher Tier H

Exam Practice

A

Without referring to previous topics and without looking at the phrases on the previous page, answer these questions. Remember to give two details in each answer or to give a reason for your answer.

1 You have broken down. Answer the garage owner's questions.
   a *Was ist mit dem Auto los?*
   b *Wo sind Sie genau?*
   c *Wann brauchen Sie das Auto wieder?*

2 You are walking in town when a car stops and the driver asks you the way.
   a *Wie komme ich am besten zum Parkhaus?*
   b *Wie weit ist es?*

3 You are staying with your German friend and are making plans for the next day. Answer your friend's questions.
   a *Was sollen wir morgen machen?*
   b *Was machst du am liebsten?*
   c *Wie ist die Wettervorhersage?*
   d *Was machen wir, wenn es regnet?*
   e *Was machst du gewöhnlich am Wochenende?*
   f *Was hast du letztes Wochenende gemacht?*
   g *Was ist dein Lieblingsfilm? Was für ein Film ist es?*
   h *Wovon handelt der Film?*
   i *Warum gefällt dir der Film so gut?*
   j *Wo und wann sollen wir uns treffen?*

B

1 Cover the teacher's role and prepare the candidate's role.
2 Then read the teacher's role.

Teacher's Role

1 Reparaturwerkstatt Schäfer. Wie kann ich Ihnen helfen? *(Candidate's task: to explain what the problem is.)*
2 Wo liegt das Problem genau? *(Candidate's task: to explain exactly what is wrong.)*
3 Das könnte ernst sein. Wo sind Sie genau? *(Candidate's task: to explain exactly where the car is.)*
4 Wir machen in zwei Stunden zu. Was möchten Sie machen? *(Candidate's task: to say what he/she is going to do.)*
5 Ist in Ordnung.

Candidate's Role

You have almost reached Hamburg to catch a ferry when your car breaks down. You need help urgently so you phone a garage.
1 Problem
2 Details des Problems
3 Auto – wo?
4 !

Your teacher will play the part of the garage owner and will speak first.

(AQA/NEAB – 1998)

3 In the model answer below, the phrases are not in the correct order. Re-order the phrases and write out the completed dialogue.
4 Compare it with your own dialogue. Change your own dialogue if necessary. Practise it with your partner and learn it.
5 Take it in turns to take the part of the teacher. Change the order of the teacher's questions so that you get used to answering them in any order.

Model Answer

– Das ist ernst. Wo sind Sie genau?
– Reparaturwerkstatt Schäfer. Wie kann ich Ihnen helfen?
– Ist in Ordnung.
– **Ich bin auf der Bundestraße zwischen Bonn und Köln. Ich bin drei Kilometer von Bonn enfernt**.
– Wo liegt das Problem genau?
– Wir machen in zwei Stunden zu. Was möchten Sie machen?
– **Ich habe eine Panne**.
– **Könnten Sie einen Mechaniker schicken? Ich warte hier im Auto**.
– **Es gibt ein komisches Geräusch im Motor**.

Shopping

Foundation Tier & Foundation/Higher Tier — F&F/H

Welches Geschäft? / Which shop?

Gibt es eine Bäckerei in der Nähe?	Is there a baker's near here?
Wo gibt es eine Apotheke? Wo kann ich Milch kaufen?	Where is there a chemist's? Where can I buy milk?
Wann macht der Supermarkt auf?	When does the supermarket open?
Wann macht die Metzgerei zu?	When does the butcher's close?
Das Kaufhaus macht um acht Uhr dreißig auf.	The department store opens at 8.30.

Einkäufe machen / Going shopping

Bitte sehr?	Can I help you?
Ich möchte eine Flasche Mineralwasser, bitte.	I would like a bottle of mineral water, please.
Haben Sie Brötchen?	Have you got any bread rolls?
Leider haben wir kein Brot.	Unfortunately, we have no bread.
Fünfhundert Gramm Käse/Ein Kilo Äpfel, bitte.	500 grams of cheese/A kilo of apples, please.
Ein Pfund Tomaten/Ein Stück Torte, bitte.	A pound of tomatoes/A piece of gâteau, please.
Ist das alles?	Is that all?
Nein, eine Packung Kekse, bitte.	No, a packet of biscuits, please.
Was kosten die Apfelsinen?	What do the oranges cost?
Sie kosten siebzig Pfennig das Stück.	They cost 70 Pfennig each.
Eine kleine Dose Suppe/Eine Schachtel Pralinen bitte.	A small tin of soup/A box of chocolates, please.
Sonst noch etwas?	Anything else?
Verkaufen Sie Obst?	Do you sell fruit?
Was macht das zusammen?	What does that cost all together?

Kleidung kaufen / Buying clothes

Ich suche ein Geschenk für meinen Bruder.	I'm looking for a present for my brother.
Ich suche eine Hose aus Baumwolle.	I'm looking for a pair of cotton trousers.
Welche Farbe möchten Sie?	What colour would you like?
Haben Sie diese Jacke in Schwarz?	Have you got this jacket in black?
Welche Größe?	What size?
Mittelgroß.	Medium.
Kann ich bitte diese Schuhe anprobieren?	May I try on these shoes?
Sie sind mir zu klein. Das Hemd ist mir zu groß.	They are too small for me. The shirt is too big for me.
Haben Sie etwas Kleineres?	Have you got anything smaller?
Was kostet das in Euro?	What does it cost in Euros?
Das ist zu teuer.	It is too expensive.
Haben Sie etwas Billigeres?	Have you got anything cheaper?
Ich mag diesen Pullover sehr.	I like this pullover a lot.
Ich nehme diese Sonnenbrille.	I'll take these sunglasses.

Du kaufst in einem kleinen Dorf in Österreich ein.

[Cartoon dialogue:]
- Bitte sehr?
- Ich möchte fünfhundert Gramm Schinken, bitte.
- Sonst noch etwas?
- Was kosten die Pfirsiche, bitte?
- Sie kosten zwei Schilling das Stück.
- Zwei Pfirsiche, bitte.
- Ist das alles?
- Nein – verkaufen Sie Brot?
- Ja.
- Fünf Brötchen, bitte.
- Was macht das zusammen?
- Das macht fünfundzwanzig Schilling, bitte.

1. Practise the dialogue with your partner until you know it really well.
2. Using the instructions below, Partner A covers the cartoon and acts the part of the young man. Partner B plays the part of the shopkeeper, reading the lines from the cartoon.
   - Say you would like 500 grams of ham. • Ask the price of the peaches. • Ask for two peaches.
   - Ask if they sell bread. • Ask for five bread rolls. • Ask what the total price is.

Foundation Tier & Foundation/Higher Tier **F&F/H**

Exam Practice

> *Exam Tip*
> - Be careful with the role-plays in this topic. You will always need to use *Sie* to the shop assistant, e.g. *Haben Sie Tomaten? Haben Sie etwas Billigeres?*

Shopping list:
- 1 bottle of Coca Cola
- 2 packets of tea
- 1 packet of chewing gum
- 250g cheese
- 1 tin of cherries

F **A**
1. Translate this shopping list into German. If there are any words you do not know, look them up in the glossary at the back of this book.
2. Without looking at the previous page, write a dialogue in which you buy all the things on your list. Act out your dialogue with your partner.

F **B**
1. Write the role-play below in full.

Teacher's Role	Candidate's Role
Du bist in einem Kaufhaus in Deutschland. Ich bin der/die Verkäufer/Verkäuferin. 1 Guten Tag. Bitte sehr? 2 Welche Farbe möchten Sie? 3 Wie gefällt Ihnen dieser Pullover? 4 Hundert Euro. 5 Leider habe ich nichts Billigeres.	You are in a department store in Germany. 1 Say you want to buy a jumper. 2 Say you want a black and white one. 3 Ask how much it is in Euros. 4 Say that it is too expensive. Your teacher will play the part of the shop assistant and will speak first.

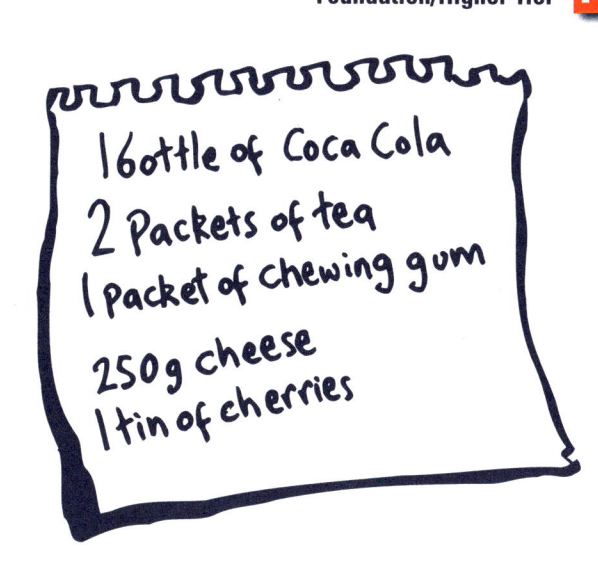

(Adapted from AQA/NEAB)

2. Now write two more role-plays in which you buy a different item of clothing in a different colour. Practise all three role-plays with your partner.

F/H **C**
1. In the role-play below, cover the teacher's role. What unexpected question do you think the teacher will ask? Prepare your answer to that question.
2. Uncover the teacher's role and practise the role-play with your partner.

> *Exam Tip*
> - In this topic, you should be able to predict quite easily what question your teacher will ask at the **!** task. Be ready to state quantities, sizes and colours. You should also be prepared to say whether you like something and how it fits.
> - Be careful to use the correct phrase to express your like or dislike of something, i.e.
> *Ich mag* = I like; *Ich mag nicht* = I don't like (*Ich möchte* = I would like, <u>not</u> I like.)

Teacher's Role	Candidate's Role
1 Guten Tag. Bitte sehr? 2 Welche Farbe und welche Größe möchten Sie? 3 Wie gefällt Ihnen der Mantel? 4 Probieren Sie diesen Mantel an. Er ist kleiner. 5 Schön.	You are in a department store in Germany and have seen a coat you like. 1 Tell the shop assistant you would like to try on this coat. 2 ! 3 Tell him/her it is too big. 4 Tell him/her that you like the coat very much. Your teacher will play the part of the shop assistant and will speak first.

47

Shopping

Higher Tier H

Einkäufe machen
Wo ist die Herrenabteilung?
In welchem Stock kann ich eine Brieftasche kaufen?
Lederwaren sind im Erdgeschoss.
Ich schaue mich nur um.
Haben Sie dieselbe Krawatte in Blau?
Ich nehme es nicht. Es ist mir zu teuer.
Ich gehe nicht gern einkaufen.
Am Samstag sind die Geschäfte zu voll.
Ich gehe lieber am Sonntag einkaufen.

Going shopping
Where is the men's department?
On what floor can I buy a wallet?
Leather goods are on the ground floor.
I'm just looking.
Have you got the same tie in blue?
I won't take it. It is too expensive.
I don't like going shopping.
On Saturdays the shops are too crowded.
I prefer to go shopping on Sunday.

Probleme beim Einkaufen
Ich habe diesen Pullover gestern für meine Freundin gekauft.
Gibt es ein Problem?
Er passt ihr/ihm nicht. Er ist ihr/ihm zu groß.
Er hat die CD schon selber gekauft.
Kann ich sie umtauschen, bitte? Es funktioniert nicht richtig.
Es gibt hier ein Loch. Es ist hier schmutzig.
Ich habe die Quittung noch.
Könnten Sie es ersetzen, bitte?
Ich möchte mein Geld zurück, bitte.
Ich möchte mit Ihrem Chef sprechen.

Shopping problems
I bought this pullover yesterday for my friend.
Is there a problem?
It doesn't fit her/him. It is too big for her/him.
He has already bought the CD himself.
May I exchange it, please? It doesn't work properly.
There is a hole here. It is dirty here.
I've still got the receipt.
Could you replace it, please?
I would like my money back, please.
I would like to speak with your boss.

Deine deutsche Freundin hat gestern ein Geschenk für deinen kleinen Bruder gekauft. Leider funktioniert es nicht richtig. Du gehst ins Geschäft zurück.

Panel 1:
- Kann ich Ihnen helfen?
- Wo ist die <u>Spielzeugabteilung</u>, bitte?

Panel 2:
- Bitte sehr?
- Meine Freundin hat dieses <u>Spielzeug</u> <u>gestern</u> gekauft.

Panel 3:
- Gibt es ein Problem?
- Ja, es funktioniert nicht richtig.

Panel 4:
- Könnten Sie es bitte ersetzen?
- Leider haben wir diese <u>Spielzeuge</u> nicht mehr.

Panel 5:
- Dann möchte ich bitte das Geld zurück.
- Haben Sie die Quittung?

Panel 6:
- Ja, hier habe ich die Quittung.
- Gut. Einen Augenblick, bitte.

1. Copy out only the assistant's part from the dialogue above. Now write the customer's part using the following instructions:

   Your friend bought a toy yesterday for your little brother. Unfortunately it does not work. You still have the receipt and you go back to the department store to replace it.

2. Now change the underlined words in the cartoon dialogue to create a new dialogue to match the following instructions:

   Your friend bought a CD for your sister yesterday. Unfortunately, your sister already has this CD. You go to the department store and try to replace the CD.

48

Higher Tier H

Exam Practice

A
Cover the previous page and see how many more sentences you can write for each cue word below.

Was? Ich habe diesen Ring für meine Freundin gekauft.
Wann? Ich habe diesen Ring gestern Nachmittag gekauft.
Wo? Ich habe diesen Ring in diesem Geschäft gekauft.
Problem? Der Ring ist ihr zu klein.
Lösung? Könnten Sie ihn bitte umtauschen?

B
1 Cover the teacher's role and prepare the candidate's role below.
2 Now read the teacher's role. Practise the whole role-play with your partner, taking it in turns to take the part of the teacher and the candidate.
3 Finally, read the model answer. Compare it with your dialogue. Notice how each answer is detailed enough to score four marks. Adapt your dialogue if necessary, write it out and learn it.

> *Exam Tip*
> - Usually in this sort of role-play, you will only be told what you have bought and that there is a problem. You will not be given details of the problem. You will need therefore to prepare a simple explanation of the problem, and be ready either to ask for the item to be exchanged or to ask for your money back.
> - Be prepared also to answer a question from another topic, as in the third task of the role-play below.

Teacher's Role
1 Bitte sehr? *(Candidate's task: to say that he/she wants to change the T-shirt.)*
2 Gibt es ein Problem? *(Candidate's task: to give a reason for wanting to change the shirt.)*
3 Können Sie die Verkäuferin beschreiben, die Sie bedient hat? *(Candidate's task: to describe the assistant who served him/her.)*
4 Ich kenne sie nicht. Leider habe ich diese T-Shirts nicht mehr. *(Candidate's task: to offer an alternative suggestion.)*
5 Kein Problem.

Candidate's Role
You have bought a T-shirt for your friend in Germany. You go back to change the T-shirt.
1 *Problem*
2 *Details des Problems*
3 *Beschreibung der Verkäuferin*
4 !
Your teacher will play the part of the shop assistant and will speak first.

(Adapted from AQA/NEAB)

Model Answer
– Bitte sehr?
– **Ich habe dieses T-Shirt für meinen Freund gekauft. Ich möchte es umtauschen, bitte.**
– Gibt es ein Problem?
– **Ja, es gibt hier ein Loch.**
– Können Sie die Verkäuferin beschreiben, die Sie bedient hat?
– **Sie ist ungefähr dreißig Jahre alt. Sie ist klein und sie hat blonde Haare.**
– Ich kennne sie nicht. Leider habe ich diese T-Shirts nicht mehr.
– **Dann möchte ich mein Geld zurück, bitte. Ich habe die Quittung noch.**
– Kein Problem.

C
The pictures below show things you have bought which you want to exchange. Write a dialogue in which you try to exchange each item or get your money back.

Public Services

Foundation Tier & Foundation/Higher Tier F&F/H

Auf der Post
Wo ist die nächste Post?
Wo ist der Briefkasten, bitte?
Ich möchte diese Ansichtskarten nach England schicken.
Was kostet es, einen Brief nach Großbritannien zu schicken?
Zwei Briefmarken zu einer Mark, bitte.
Verkaufen Sie Briefmarken? Ich brauche Briefmarken für Schottland.

At the post office
Where is the nearest post office?
Where is the letter box, please?
I would like to send these postcards to England.
What does it cost to send a letter to Great Britain?
Two stamps at DM 1, please.
Do you sell stamps? I need stamps for Scotland.

Am Telefon
Gibt es in der Nähe ein Telefon?
Können Sie einen Zwanzigmarkschein wechseln?
Haben Sie Kleingeld?
Ich brauche Münzen für das Telefon.
Wie ist Ihre Telefonnummer?
Meine Nummer ist dreiundachtzig zweiundzwanzig sechzehn.
Wie ist die Vorwahl?
Hallo. Schäfer.
Ich möchte mit Herrn Schmidt sprechen, bitte.
Am Apparat.
Ist Susi da?
Einen Augenblick, bitte.
Leider ist Frau Braun im Moment nicht da.
Wer spricht?
Kann ich ihr etwas ausrichten?
Können Sie ihr sagen, dass John angerufen hat?
Kann sie mich zurückrufen?
Wann kann sie Sie zurückrufen?
Heute Nachmittag um drei Uhr. Auf Wiederhören.

On the phone
Is there a telephone near here?
Can you change a twenty Mark note?
Have you got any change?
I need coins for the phone.
What is your telephone number?
My number is 832216.
What is the dialling code?
Hello. Schäfer speaking.
I would like to speak to Mr. Schmidt, please.
Speaking.
Is Susi there?
One moment, please.
Unfortunately, Mrs Braun isn't here at the moment.
Who's speaking?
Can I give her a message?
Can you tell her that John phoned?
Can she phone me back?
When can she phone you back?
This afternoon at three o'clock. Good-bye (on the phone).

Du kaufst Ansichtskarten in einem kleinen Geschäft in der Schweiz.

A
- Bitte sehr?
- ... Sie ... ?
- Ja.
- Drei ... für diese ... nach ... , bitte ...
- Vor dem Geschäft.

Du möchtest mit Fräulein Fischer sprechen. Du rufst sie im Büro an.

B
- Schäfer.
- Guten Tag. Ich m ... m ... Fräulein Fischer s ... , bitte.
- Fräulein Fischer ist leider nicht da. Kann ich ihr etwas ausrichten?
- Ja. K ... S ... ihr s ..., d ... Frau Schwarz a ... h ... ?
- Sehr gut, Frau Schwarz. Wann kann sie Sie zurückrufen?
- H ... A ... gegen z ... U ... , bitte.

1. Write the dialogue in cartoon **A** in full.
2. Write a new dialogue in which you buy stamps for four letters to England.
3. Now write the dialogue in cartoon **B** in full.
4. Practise both dialogues with your partner. Use only the gapped dialogues on this page to help you.

**Foundation Tier &
Foundation/Higher Tier** F&F/H

Exam Practice

F A

1 Look at the role-play instructions below and prepare what you would say.
2 Practise the role-play with your partner until you can perform it from memory.

Teacher's Role	Candidate's Role
Du bist in einem Laden in Deutschland. Ich bin der Verkäufer/die Verkäuferin. 1 Bitte sehr? 2 Sonst noch etwas? 3 Ja, aber nur für Ansichtskarten. 4 Bitte sehr. 5 Hier rechts.	You are in a shop in Germany. 1 Say you want four postcards. 2 Ask if they sell stamps. 3 Say you want stamps for England. 4 Ask where the letter box is. Your teacher will play the part of the shop assistant and will speak first.

(Adapted from AQA/NEAB)

F/H B

1 In your Foundation/Higher Tier role-play you will always have to answer a question which is shown by a ! task.
  Answer each of the questions below.
  a Was für Briefmarken möchten Sie?
  b Wie ist Ihre Telefonnummer? (*Write your answer in words, not numbers.*)
  c Wie ist die Vorwahl?
  d Wer spricht? Wie schreibt man das, bitte? (*Remember you must be able to spell your name. The German alphabet is on page 7.*)
  e Kann ich ihm etwas ausrichten?
  f Wann kann er Sie zurückrufen?
2 Now practise the role-play with your partner. Take it in turns to play the part of the candidate. Then write out the role-play and learn it.

> *Exam Tip*
> - In the role-play below, the unexpected question does not come from the list of phrases for this topic. If this happens in your exam, make your answer as simple as possible. Try to think of something you can say easily in German. Don't try and translate a difficult English answer.
> - Here are some easy answers which will score good marks: *Meine Mutter hat Geburtstag./Mein Großvater ist krank./Ich möchte meine Freundin treffen. /Ich kann meinen Freund nicht treffen.*

Teacher's Role	Candidate's Role
1 Was ist los? 2 Kein Problem. 3 In der nächsten Straße. 4 Ja. Warum musst du einen Anruf machen? 5 Schon gut. Also bis später.	You are in a town in Germany with your German friend. 1 Tell him/her that you need to make a phone call. 2 Ask him/her where there is a telephone box. 3 Ask if he/she can change a 10 Mark note. 4 ! Your teacher will play the part of your friend and will speak first.

(Adapted from AQA/NEAB)

Public Services

Higher Tier — H

Am Telefon
Sie können mich per Fax erreichen.
Wo kann ich eine Telefonkarte kaufen?
Kann ich es per E-mail schicken?

On the phone
You can reach me by fax.
Where can I buy a phone card?
Can I send it by e-mail?

Auf der Post
Ich möchte dieses Paket in die USA schicken.
Was kostet es, dieses Paket nach Österreich zu schicken?
Ich möchte es per Luftpost schicken.
Sie müssen dieses Formular ausfüllen.

At the post office
I'd like to send this parcel to the U.S.A.
What does it cost to send this parcel to Austria?
I'd like to send it by air mail.
You must fill in this form.

Geld wechseln
Ich möchte fünfzig Pfund in Euro wechseln.
Wie ist heute der Kurs für das Pfund?
Kann ich hier Reiseschecks einlösen, bitte?
Ich möchte keine großen Scheine.
Kann ich diesen Zwanzigmarkschein in Münzen wechseln, bitte?
Wo muss ich unterschreiben?
Haben Sie ein Fünfzigpfennigstück?

Changing money
I'd like to change £50 into Euros.
What is the rate of exchange for the pound today?
Can I cash traveller's cheques here, please?
I don't want any large notes.
Can I change this twenty Mark note into coins, please?
Where must I sign?
Have you got a fifty Pfennig coin?

Im Fundbüro
Ich habe meinen Koffer verloren.
Wann haben Sie ihn verloren?
Ich habe ihn heute Morgen gegen zehn Uhr verloren.
Wo haben Sie ihn verloren?
Ich habe ihn im Zug liegen lassen.
Ich kann mein Portemonnaie nicht finden.
Vielleicht hat es jemand gestohlen.
Können Sie die Tasche beschreiben?
Sie ist klein und braun und aus Leder.
Mein Name ist darin.
In der Tasche waren meine Scheckkarte, meine Schlüssel und mein Portemonnaie.
Hat jemand meine Jacke gefunden?
Was soll ich machen?
Wie kann ich Sie am besten erreichen?
Sie können mich anrufen.

At the lost property office
I have lost my case.
When did you lose it?
I lost it this morning at about ten o'clock.
Where did you lose it?
I left it in the train.
I can't find my purse.
Perhaps someone has stolen it.
Can you describe the bag?
It is small and brown and made of leather.
My name is in it.
In the bag were my cheque card, my keys and my purse.
Has anyone found my jacket?
What should I do?
How can I best contact you?
You can phone me.

**Du hast heute Morgen deine Tasche in der Straßenbahn liegen lassen.
Du gehst zum Fundbüro.**

Panel 1: Kann ich Ihnen helfen?

Panel 2: Wann haben Sie sie verloren? — I ... h ... s ... h ... M ... v ...

Panel 3: Und wo?

Panel 4: Können Sie die Tasche — S ... i ... z ... g ... und sch ... Sie ist a ... Pl ...

Panel 5: Was war darin? — ANDY BROWN

Panel 6: W ... s ... i ... m ...? — Sie müssen dieses Formular ausfüllen.

1. Write the dialogue above in full.
2. Adapt the dialogue to report the loss of a case which you left on the train yesterday afternoon. It was a small blue case. It contained clothes, a pair of shoes, a magazine and a walkman.

52

Higher Tier H

Exam Practice

A
Which of these cue words matches which answer? Copy each cue word together with the correct answer below. Then write one additional answer for each cue word.

| Paket | £100 | Kleingeld | Geld |

- Ich möchte hundert Pfund in Schillinge wechseln.
- Ich möchte nur Zwanzigmarkscheine.
- Ich möchte dieses Paket nach Frankreich schicken.
- Haben Sie mëunzen fëur das telefon?

> *Exam Tip*
> - Be prepared again to spell your name for this topic.
> - Also be prepared to give your telephone number, including the dialling code.

B
Write four different answers to each question below.
1. Was haben Sie verloren? (*Start your answer with* Ich habe *and end it with* verloren.)
2. Wann haben Sie es verloren? (*Give time of day and an approximate time on the clock.*)
3. Wo haben Sie es verloren? (*Say exactly where, e.g. if you lost it in the train, state the destination of the train.*)
4. Können Sie es bitte beschreiben? (*Give two details. These could be colour, size, shape or what it was made of.*)
5. Was war darin? (*State at least three things in it.*)

> *Exam Tip*
> Always read the English instructions carefully. They will give you details which you must include in your answer. You should expect to be told what you have lost. You may also be told where and when you lost it.

C
1. Cover the teacher's role and prepare the candidate's role below. Remember either to answer in a full sentence or to give more than one detail in your answer.
2. Now read what the teacher is going to ask you. Check your answers and write your answer to each question including the ! task.

Teacher's Role	**Candidate's Role**
1 Wie kann ich Ihnen helfen? 2 Können Sie den Koffer bitte beschreiben? Was war darin? 3 Wo und wann haben Sie den Koffer zum letzten Mal gesehen? 4 Wie heißen Sie, bitte? Können Sie das buchstabieren? Wie kann ich Sie erreichen? 5 Wenn jemand den Koffer findet, rufe ich Sie an.	You have lost your suitcase and you go to a lost property office. 1 *Problem* 2 *Beschreibung und Inhalt* 3 *Wo und wann?* 4 ! Your teacher will play the part of the clerk and will speak first.

(Adapted from AQA/NEAB)

3. Below is an example of one candidate's answers. Read the answers together with the notes which show what you must do to gain full marks. Where has this candidate lost marks? Write out the role-play again so that all the answers gain four marks.

Model Answer
– Wie kann ich Ihnen helfen? (*Candidate's task: to state what he/she has lost.*)
– **Ich habe meinen Koffer verloren**.
– Können Sie den Koffer bitte beschreiben? Was war darin? (*Candidate's task: to describe the case and contents with at least four details.*)
– **Er ist schwarz. Mein Name ist darin**.
– Wo und wann haben Sie den Koffer zum letzten Mal gesehen? (*Candidate's task: to say when and where he/she last saw the case.*)

– **Am Bahnhof**.
– Wie heißen Sie, bitte? Können Sie das buchstabieren? Wie kann ich Sie erreichen? (*Candidate's task: to give surname, spell it and say how he/she can be contacted.*)
– **Brown. B-R-O-W-N.**
– Wenn jemand den Koffer findet, rufe ich Sie an.

53

Travel

Foundation Tier & Foundation/Higher Tier — F&F/H

In die Stadt fahren / Travelling to town

Wie komme ich am besten in die Stadt?	How do I best get into town?
Am besten fahren Sie mit dem Bus.	It's best to go by bus.
Sie können auch mit der Straßenbahn fahren.	You can also go by tram.
Es ist billiger mit dem Bus.	It is cheaper by bus.
Wie oft fährt der Bus?	How often does the bus go?
Alle zehn Minuten.	Every ten minutes.
Wo ist die Haltestelle?	Where is the bus stop?
Welche Linie fährt zum Bahnhof?	Which number bus goes to the station?
Fährt dieser Bus zum Dom?	Does this bus go to the cathedral?
Sie müssen mit der Linie zwei fahren.	You must go on the number two.

Mit dem Zug fahren / Travelling by train

Wann fährt ein Zug nach Dresden?	When does a train go to Dresden?
Wann möchten Sie fahren?	When do you want to travel?
Morgen Nachmittag gegen zwei Uhr.	Tomorrow afternoon at about two o'clock.
Ich möchte morgen früh fahren.	I would like to travel tomorrow morning.
Es gibt einen Zug um zehn Uhr.	There is a train at 10.00.
Wann fährt der nächste Zug nach Wien?	When does the next train go to Vienna?
Er fährt um sechzehn Uhr.	It goes at 16.00.
Wann kommt er in Bonn an?	When does it arrive in Bonn?
Er kommt um sechzehn Uhr dreißig an.	It arrives at 16.30.
Von welchem Gleis fährt er nach Bern?	From which platform does it leave for Bern?
Muss ich umsteigen?	Do I have to change?

Fahrkarten kaufen / Buying tickets

Wo kann ich eine Fahrkarte kaufen?	Where can I buy a ticket?
Gibt es einen Fahrkartenautomat?	Is there a ticket machine?
Einfach, oder hin und zurück?	Single or return?
Einmal nach München, hin und zurück.	One to Munich, return.
Eine Rückfahrkarte nach München, bitte.	A return ticket to Munich, please.
Zweimal nach Köln, einfach.	Two to Cologne, single.
Zwei einfache Fahrkarten nach Köln.	Two single tickets to Cologne.
Welcher Klasse?	Which class?
Erster/zweiter Klasse.	First/second class.
Ich möchte mit einem Intercityzug fahren.	I would like to go on an intercity train.
Muss ich Zuschlag bezahlen?	Do I have to pay a supplement?

Du möchtest heute mit dem Zug nach Berlin fahren. Du gehst zur Auskunft.

A: [BERLIN ?] — Er fährt um dreizehn Uhr. — [BERLIN ?] — Er kommt um fünfzehn Uhr zwanzig an. — Gleis? — Von Gleis sieben.

Du fährst heute nach Frankfurt. Du kaufst eine Fahrkarte.

B: Guten Tag. Bitte sehr? — Frankfurt. — Einfach, oder hin und zurück? — Welcher Klasse? — 2

1. Write out these two role-plays in full.
2. Adapt the role-plays to complete these tasks.

   You are at a station in Germany:
   - Ask what time the next train goes to Cologne.
   - Ask for two tickets to Cologne.
   - Say you want single tickets.
   - Ask what platform you need.

Foundation Tier & Foundation/Higher Tier F&F/H

Exam Practice

A
Complete the two role-plays below.

Role-play 1

Teacher's Role

Du bist auf einem Verkehrsamt. Ich bin der Beamte/die Beamtin.
1 Bitte sehr?
2 Am besten fahren Sie mit dem Bus.
3 Sie müssen mit der Linie drei fahren.
4 Alle zwanzig Minuten.
5 Dort rechts.

Candidate's Role

You are in an information office in a German town.

1 Ask the best way to the sports centre.
2 Ask what number bus to take.
3 Ask how often the bus goes.
4 Ask where the bus stop is.

Your teacher will play the part of the official and will speak first.

Role-play 2

Teacher's Role

Du bist auf einem Bahnhof. Ich bin der Beamte/die Beamtin.
1 Bitte sehr?
2 Wann möchten Sie fahren?
3 Um wie viel Uhr?
4 Es gibt einen Zug um neun Uhr dreißig.
5 Dreihundert Schilling.

Candidate's Role

You are at a station in Germany.

1 Ask when there is a train to Vienna.
2 Say you want to go tomorrow morning.
3 Say you want to go at about 9 o'clock.
4 Ask for a return ticket to Vienna.

Your teacher will play the part of the official and will speak first.

B
1 Practise this role-play with your partner. Take it in turns to take the candidate's role.
2 Make a new role-play by changing as many details as possible, e.g. where you want to go, when you want to travel. Act out your role-play. Can the rest of the class notice the changes you have made?

Teacher's Role

1 Bitte sehr?
2 Wann möchten Sie genau fahren?
3 Es gibt einen Intercityzug um vierzehn Uhr.
4 Nein, mit diesem Zug nicht. Was für Fahrkarten möchten Sie und wie viele?
5 Bitte sehr.

Candidate's Role

You are at a station in Germany.
1 Tell the official you want to go to Bonn today.
2 Say you want to travel this afternoon.
3 Ask if you have to pay a supplement.
4 !

Your teacher will play the part of the official and will speak first.

Travel

Higher Tier H

Reisevorbereitungen / Making travel arrangements

Ich möchte einen Platz für Samstag reservieren.	I'd like to reserve a seat for Saturday.
In einem Nichtraucherabteil.	In a no-smoking compartment.
Ich möchte einen Fensterplatz.	I'd like a window seat.
Mein Zug hat Verspätung.	My train is late.
Ich habe meinen Zug verpasst.	I've missed my train.
Wann geht der nächste Flug nach Berlin?	When is the next flight to Berlin?
Wann landet er in Berlin?	When does it land in Berlin?

Meinungen äußern / Expressing opinions

Ich fliege gern. Es ist praktisch und auch schnell.	I like flying. It is practical and it is also fast.
Ich fahre nicht gern mit dem Schiff.	I don't like travelling by ship.
Ich fahre lieber durch den Tunnel, weil ich seekrank werde.	I prefer to go through the tunnel, because I get seasick.
Man sollte mit dem Rad fahren.	People should go by bike.
Es ist nicht so schmutzig wie das Auto.	It is not as dirty as a car.
Es ist umweltfreundlicher.	It is better for the environment.

Ein Unfall / An accident

Es ist ein Unfall passiert.	There has been an accident.
Was ist passiert?	What happened?
Ein Auto ist zu schnell gefahren.	A car went too quickly.
Es hat an der Ampel nicht gehalten.	It didn't stop at the traffic lights.
Es ist ins Schleudern gekommen.	It skidded.
Es hat eine Frau überfahren.	It has run a woman over.
Das Auto hat ein Mädchen umgefahren.	The car has knocked down a girl.
Ein Kind ist vom Rad gefallen.	A child has fallen from his bike.
Ist jemand verletzt?	Is anyone injured?
Der alte Mann ist verletzt.	The old man is injured.
Er hat sich vielleicht das Bein gebrochen.	He has perhaps broken his leg.
Sie ist am Kopf verletzt. Wir brauchen einen Krankenwagen.	She has a head injury. We need an ambulance.
Wo sind Sie genau?	Where are you exactly?
Ich bin an der Kreuzung der Kirchstraße und der Bahnhofstraße.	I am at the crossroads of Church Road and Station Road.

Du sprichst mit deinem Freund über die Ferien.

A: Wie fährst du normalerweise in Urlaub? — Warum? — Fährst du nie mit dem Schiff? — Nein, weil ... ...

Du bist in der Stadt und du hast gerade einen Unfall gesehen. Du rufst die Polizei an.

B: Wie kann ich Ihnen helfen? — Was ist passiert? — Ist jemand verletzt?

1. Complete the two role-plays above.
2. Practise the role-plays with your partner. Partner A covers the role-plays and uses only the cues below to answer partner B's questions. Take it in turns to answer the questions using the cues.
Partner A: Urlaub Grund Schiff
Partner B: Problem Details Verletzte

Higher Tier H

Exam Practice

A

1 Read the cues below, then read the candidate's answers. Which answer matches which cue?

Cues		Candidate's answers	
i	Verletzte	a	Ich möchte einen Platz reservieren.
ii	Fliegen	b	Ich fahre gern durch den Tunnel.
iii	Details	c	Ein Junge ist verletzt.
iv	Platz	d	Es ist ein Unfall passiert.
v	Tunnel	e	Ich fliege gern.

2 In the examples above, the candidate only gave short answers and therefore did not score the full four marks. Add something to each answer to give more information.

B

1 Cover the teacher's role, read the candidate's instructions and prepare what you are going to say. What do you think the teacher will ask you for the ! task?

2 Now read the teacher's questions. Did you guess the second question correctly? Check your answers and make sure that you give enough details to score four marks.

Exam Tip
- In this role-play, important instructions are given in the English introduction. Remember to include these details when you prepare your answers. Remember to say how the two people have been injured.

Teacher's Role

1 *Polizeiwache.* (Candidate's task: to say there has been an accident.)
2 *Was ist genau passiert?* (Candidate's task: to give two details of what happened.)
3 *Ist jemand verletzt?* (Candidate's task: To describe the injuries of the two people involved in the accident.)
4 *Wo ist der Unfall genau passiert?* (Candidate's task: to describe exactly where the accident took place.)
5 *Wir werden einen Krankenwagen schicken.*

Candidate's Role

You are in Germany and you have just seen an accident. Two people have been injured. You phone the police.
1 *Problem*
2 *!*
3 *Verletzte*
4 *Wo*

Your teacher will play the part of the police officer and will speak first.

C

Complete the role-play below in the same way. Remember to add a reason whenever you are asked your opinion, e.g. *Man sollte öfter mit dem Zug fahren, weil es umweltfreundlicher ist.*

Teacher's Role

1 *Wie fährt man am besten in die nächste Stadt?* (Candidate's task: to say the best way to get to the next town.)
2 *Warum?* (Candidate's task: to say why this is the best means of transport to get to the next town.)
3 *Fliegst du gern?* (Candidate's task: To say whether he/she likes flying and why.)
4 *Ich fahre lieber mit dem Schiff. Fährst du nicht auch lieber mit dem Schiff?* (Candidate's task: to say whether he/she prefers to go by ship and why.)
5 *Ja, du hast Recht.*

Candidate's Role

You are visiting your friend in Germany. You make arrangements to go into the next town.
1 *die nächste Stadt*
2 *!*
3 *Flugzeug*
4 *Schiff*

Your teacher will play the part of your friend and will speak first.

57

Education & Employment

Foundation Tier & Foundation/Higher Tier F&F/H

Pläne für die Zukunft
Was machst du nächstes Jahr?
Ich bleibe auf der Schule.
Ich möchte Naturwissenschaften studieren.
Ich möchte eine Arbeitsstelle als Lehrling finden.
Möchtest du auf die Uni gehen?

Plans for the future
What are you doing next year?
I'm going to stay on at school.
I would like to study science.
I would like to find a job as an apprentice.
Would you like to go to university?

Die Arbeit
Wie kommst du zur Arbeit?
Ich fahre mit dem Bus zur Arbeit.
Die Fahrt dauert eine Viertelstunde.
Was macht dein Bruder?
Er ist arbeitslos. Er sucht eine Stelle in einem Büro.
Was ist dein Vater von Beruf?
Mein Vater arbeitet in einer Fabrik.
Arbeitet deine Mutter?
Meine Mutter ist Sekretärin.

Work
How do you get to work?
I go to work by bus.
The journey takes a quarter of an hour.
What does your brother do?
He is unemployed. He is looking for a job in an office.
What does your father do for a living?
My father works in a factory.
Does your mother work?
My mother is a secretary.

Dein Arbeitspraktikum
Hast du ein Arbeitspraktikum gemacht?
Ich habe drei Wochen in einer Grundschule gearbeitet.
Wie hat dir die Arbeit gefallen?
Die Arbeit war sehr interessant.

Your work placement
Have you done a work placement?
I worked for three weeks in a Primary School.
How did you like the work?
The work was very interesting.

Einen Job beschreiben
Hast du einen Job?
Ich trage Zeitungen aus. Samstags arbeite ich in einem Café.
Ich möchte eine Stelle als Verkäufer finden.
Ich möchte Geld verdienen.
Wie viele Stunden arbeitest du am Tag?
Ich arbeite sonntags sechs Stunden.
Mein Arbeitstag beginnt um acht Uhr.
Wie viel Geld verdienst du?
Ich verdiene vier Pfund pro Stunde.
Wie gefällt dir die Arbeit?
Die Arbeit ist langweilig, aber ich brauche das Geld.

Describing a job
Do you have a job?
I deliver newspapers. On Saturdays, I work in a café.
I would like to find a job as a sales assistant.
I would like to earn some money.
How many hours do you work in a day?
I work for six hours on Sundays.
My working day starts at eight o'clock.
How much money do you earn?
I earn £4 an hour.
How do you like the work?
The work is boring but I need the money.

Dein deutscher Freund macht eine Umfrage über die Arbeit.

- Hast du ein Arbeitspraktikum gemacht?
- Ja, ich habe drei Wochen in einem Kaufhaus gearbeitet.
- Wie hat dir die Arbeit gefallen?
- Die Arbeit war schwer aber interessant.
- Und hast du jetzt einen Job?
- Ja, ich arbeite in einem Supermarkt.
- Wie viele Stunden arbeitest du dort?
- Ich arbeite samstags sechs Stunden und sonntags fünf Stunden.
- Wie viel Geld verdienst du?
- Ich verdiene vier Pfund fünfzig pro Stunde.
- Wie gefällt dir die Arbeit?
- Die Arbeit ist langweilig.

Practise the dialogue with your partner. Then re-write it to describe your work placement and any job you have.

Exam Practice

F A

1 Work with your partner and test each other on the phrases on the previous page. Partner A says an English phrase. Partner B translates it into German. Make sure you change the order of the phrases as you test each other. This will help you to learn them.

2 Remember that you will always have to ask at least one question in your Foundation Tier role-play. Without looking at the previous page, write the following questions in German.

   a Ask if your friend has a job.
   b Ask how many hours your friend works at weekends.
   c Ask what your friend is doing next year.
   d Ask if your friend's sister works.
   e Ask what your friend would like to study.
   f Ask where your friend would like to work.

F B

Again, without looking at the previous page, write the two role-plays below in full.

Role-play 1

Teacher's Role	Candidate's Role
Du sprichst mit deinem deutschen Freund/deiner deutschen Freundin. Ich bin der Freund/die Freundin. 1 Was machst du nächstes Jahr? 2 Was für eine Stelle möchtest du? 3 Warum? 4 Du hast Recht. 5 Ich bleibe auf der Schule.	You are talking to your German friend about your plans for next year. 1 Say you want to work. 2 Say you would like to be a sales assistant. 3 Say it is an interesting job. 4 Ask what your friend is going to do next year. Your teacher will play the part of your friend and will speak first.

(Adapted from AQA/NEAB)

Role-play 2

Teacher's Role	Candidate's Role
Du sprichst mit deinem deutschen Freund/mit deiner deutschen Freundin. Ich bin der Freund/die Freundin. 1 Wo arbeitest du? 2 Was für Arbeit machst du dort? 3 Wann endet dein Arbeitstag? 4 Das ist aber spät. 5 Nein, ich arbeite nicht.	You are talking to your German friend about your job. 1 Say you work in a restaurant. 2 Say you are a waiter/waitress. 3 Say you finish at six o'clock. 4 Ask if your friend has a job. Your teacher will play the part of your friend and will speak first.

(Adapted from AQA/NEAB)

F/H C

Write the role-play below in full without looking at the previous page.

Teacher's Role	Candidate's Role
1 Was machst du im Sommer? 2 Was für eine Stelle suchst du? 3 Hast du schon gearbeitet? 4 Warum brauchst du das Geld? 5 Hoffentlich findest du eine Stelle.	You are talking to your German friend about finding a job in the summer. 1 Tell him/her you want to earn some money. 2 Tell him/her you would like to work in a café. 3 Tell him/her you worked as a waiter/waitress last summer. 4 ! Your teacher will play the part of your friend and will speak first.

(Adapted from AQA/NEAB)

Education & Employment

Higher Tier H

Fortbildung
Ich muss drei Jahren auf der Fachhochschule studieren.
Um Lehrer zu werden, muß ich auf die Uni gehen.
Ich weiß nicht genau, was ich werden möchte.

Deine Pläne für die Zukunft
Warum möchtest du Fremdsprachen studieren?
Weil ich gern ins Ausland reise.
Warum möchtest du Arzt werden?
Weil ich Naturwissenschaften einfach finde.
In den nächsten zwei Jahren muss ich fleißig arbeiten.
Nach den Prüfungen möchte ich in Urlaub fahren.
Während der Sommerferien möchte ich viel Geld verdienen.

Arbeit
Hast du schon gearbeitet?
Seit wann arbeitest du dort?
Ich arbeite seit sechs Monaten in einem Restaurant.
Ich muss die Tische decken und ich muss abspülen.
Ich habe eine Stelle als Kellnerin.
Die Arbeit ist gut bezahlt.
Die Arbeit in einem Krankenhaus ist schwer.
Ich würde es zu langweilig finden, in einem Büro zu arbeiten.
Ich möchte lieber im Freien arbeiten.

Eine Arbeitsstelle suchen
Ich suche eine Stelle als Verkäufer.
Haben Sie eine Stelle frei?
Ich habe Ihre Anzeige in der Zeitung gesehen.
Ich kann jedes Wochenende arbeiten.
Ich bin ab Anfang Juli frei.
Ich bin bis Ende August frei.
Könnten Sie mir Informationen über die Stelle schicken, bitte?
Soll ich Ihnen meinen Lebenslauf schicken?
Wie sind die Arbeitsstunden?
Wie viel würde ich pro Stunde verdienen?

Further education
I must study for three years at college.
To become a teacher I have to go to college.
I am not sure what I would like to be.

Your future plans
Why would you like to study foreign languages?
Because I like going abroad.
Why would you like to become a doctor?
Because I find science easy.
I must work hard for the next two years.
After the exams, I would like to go on holiday.
During the summer holidays, I would like to earn lots of money.

Work
Have you already worked?
How long have you been working there?
I have been working in a restaurant for six months.
I have to set the tables and I have to wash up.
I've got a job as a waitress.
The work is well-paid.
Work in a hospital is hard.
I would find it too boring to work in an office.
I would prefer to work outside.

Looking for a job
I'm looking for a job as a sales assistant.
Have you got a job available?
I saw your advert in the paper.
I can work every weekend.
I am free from the beginning of July.
I am free up to the end of August.
Could you send me information about the job, please?
Should I send you my curriculum vitae?
What are the working hours?
How much would I earn per hour?

Du möchtest einen Job für den Sommer finden. Du gehst aufs Arbeitsamt.

Frame 1: Guten Tag. Ich suche eine Stelle als Kellnerin. Ich habe Ihre Anzeige in der Zeitung gesehen. — Haben Sie schon gearbeitet?

Frame 2: Ja, ich arbeite seit einem Jahr in einem Café in England. — Und ab wann sind Sie frei?

Frame 3: Ich bin vom 15. Juli bis Ende August frei. — Gut. Können Sie bitte dieses Formular ausfüllen?

1. Practise reading this role-play with your partner.
2. Adapt the role-play to apply for a job in a shop. You have done three weeks work experience in a bank and you have been working for two years at weekends at the cash desk in a supermarket at home. You are free from the beginning of July to the 20th of August. Take it in turns to ask and answer the questions.

Higher Tier H

Exam Practice

A

In this topic, you must be prepared to answer questions about your plans for the future and about any work you have done. Prepare your answers to the questions below and learn them to use in your exam.

1 Was möchtest du nächstes Jahr machen? Warum?
2 Was möchtest du werden? Warum?
3 Was möchtest du nach den Prüfungen machen?
4 Was für eine Arbeitsstelle hast du jetzt?
5 Was musst du dort machen?
6 Wie gefällt dir diese Arbeit? Warum?

Exam Tip
- Remember that you must give detailed answers to score full marks at Higher Tier. You must either give more than one detail in your answer or you must give a reason for your answer.

B

Work with your partner to learn the phrases on the previous page. Then, without referring to them, complete the two role-plays below. Get your partner to check your answers to make sure that they are detailed enough to score full marks.

Role-play 1

Teacher's Role

1 Guten Tag. Ich bin der Chef. Wie kann ich Ihnen helfen? *(Candidate's task: to explain that he/she is enquiring about the job advertised.)*
2 Haben Sie irgendwelche Fragen über die Stelle? *(Candidate's task: to ask what the hours and wages are.)*
3 Sie müssen samstags und sonntags vier Stunden arbeiten. Sie bekommen acht Mark pro Stunde. Haben Sie schon gearbeitet? *(Candidate's task: to explain what experience he/she has.)*
4 Wann können Sie arbeiten? *(Candidate's task: to say when he/she is available for work, giving a starting and finishing date.)*
5 Füllen Sie bitte dieses Formular aus.

Candidate's Role

You have seen an advertisement for a job as a sales assistant. You go into the department store to make enquiries.
1 Grund
2 Arbeitstag und Geld
3 !
4 Wann?

Your teacher will play the part of the manager and will speak first.

(Adapted from AQA/NEAB)

Role-play 2

Teacher's Role

1 Guten Tag. Wie kann ich Ihnen helfen? *(Candidate's task: to say what kind of work he/she is looking for.)*
2 Wann können Sie arbeiten? *(Candidate's task: to give hours and days of availability for work)*
3 Haben Sie schon gearbeitet? *(Candidate's task: to give details of previous work experience.)*
4 Also, wir haben zwei Stellen frei. Es gibt eine Stelle in einem Hotel in der Stadtmitte und eine Stelle auf einem Campingplatz auf dem Land. Welche Stelle interessiert Sie mehr? Warum? *(Candidate's task: to accept one of the jobs, giving a reason.)*
5 Füllen Sie bitte dieses Formular aus.

Candidate's Role

You are talking to an agency in Germany about the possibility of holiday work.
1 Was für Arbeit?
2 Arbeitstage und Stunden
3 Erfahrung
4 !

Your teacher will play the part of the employee and will speak first.

(Adapted from AQA/NEAB)

Tourism

Foundation Tier & Foundation/Higher Tier F&F/H

Meine Ferien | My holidays

Was machst du in den Ferien?	What do you do in the holidays?
Wir bleiben oft zu Hause.	We often stay at home.
Wohin fährst du in Urlaub?	Where do you go on holiday?
Wir fahren oft ans Meer.	We often go to the seaside.
Im Sommer fahren wir normalerweise ins Ausland.	We usually go abroad in summer.
Wie fährst du dorthin?	How do you travel?
Wir fahren mit dem Auto.	We travel by car.
Mit wem fährst du?	Who do you go with?
Ich fahre mit meinen Eltern.	I go with my parents.
Wie lange bleibst du dort?	How long do you stay there?
Wir bleiben oft zwei Wochen dort.	We often stay there for two weeks.
Wir wohnen oft auf einem Campingplatz.	We often stay on a campsite.
Wir gehen schwimmen. Wir wandern.	We go swimming. We go walking.
Manchmal machen wir einen Ausflug.	Sometimes, we go on an excursion.
Was machst du abends?	What do you do in the evenings?

Meine letzten Ferien | My last holidays

Wohin bist du letztes Jahr in Urlaub gefahren?	Where did you go on holiday last year?
Letzten Sommer war ich in Deutschland.	Last summer, I was in Germany.
Letztes Jahr bin ich Ski gefahren.	Last year, I went skiing.
Wie bist du dorthin gefahren?	How did you get there?
Wir sind mit dem Zug dorthin gefahren.	We went there by train.
Wir sind hingeflogen.	We flew there.
Mit wem warst du dort?	Who did you go with?
Ich war mit meiner Familie dort.	I was there with my family.
Wie lange warst du dort?	How long were you there?
Wir waren eine Woche dort.	We were there for a week.
Wir haben in einer Ferienwohnung gewohnt.	We stayed in a holiday apartment.
Wir sind jeden Tag zum Strand gegangen.	We went to the beach every day.
Was hast du gemacht?	What did you do?
Wir haben uns gesonnt. Wir haben einen Ausflug gemacht.	We sunbathed. We went on an excursion.
Wie war das Wetter?	What was the weather like?
Das Wetter war sehr schön. Es hat nicht geregnet.	The weather was lovely. It didn't rain.

Meinungen äußern | Expressing opinions

Was machst du gern in den Ferien?	What do you like to do in the holidays?
Ich fahre gern an die See.	I like going to the sea.
Die Landschaft war wunderbar.	The scenery was wonderful.
Wir waren im Museum. Es war interessant.	We went to a museum. It was interesting.
Was machst du nächsten Sommer?	What are you going to do next summer?
Ich fahre ins Ausland. Das Wetter ist schöner als hier.	I am going abroad. The weather is better than it is here.

Du sprichst mit deiner Freundin über die Ferien.

Wohin fährst du normalerweise in Urlaub? — *Wir fahren oft in die Türkei.*

Wie fährst du dorthin? — *Wir fliegen hin.*

Und was machst du dort? — *Wir gehen schwimmen und wir sonnen uns.*

1. Take it in turns to ask and answer the questions with your partner.
2. Write a new dialogue. This time the boy normally goes to Scotland for his holidays.
3. Now adapt the dialogue to say what you normally do for your holidays. Then change it to talk about what you did last year. Remember, you will have to change the questions, too, e.g. *Wohin bist du letztes Jahr in Urlaub gefahren?*

Exam Practice

Foundation Tier & Foundation/Higher Tier

A

1 Cover up the model dialogue on the right and allow yourself only three minutes to prepare the role-play.
2 Uncover the model dialogue and write it in full.
3 Practise it with a partner until you are both word perfect.

Candidate's Role

You are talking to your German friend about your holidays.
1 Say you often stay on a campsite.
2 Say it sometimes rains.
3 Say you hike and you swim.
4 Ask what your friend is going to do next summer.

Your teacher will play the part of your friend and will speak first.

Model Dialogue

Du sprichst mit deinem deutschen Freund/deiner deutschen Freundin. Ich bin der Freund/die Freundin.
1 Was machst du im Sommer?
– W … w … o … a … e … C …
2 Wie ist das Wetter?
– E … r … m …
3 Was machst du dann?
– I … w … u … i … s …
4 Schön.
– W … m … d … n … S … ?
5 Wir fahren ins Ausland.

B

1 Before you complete the role-play, write the questions below in German.
Do not look at the previous page!
Example: Ask where your friend normally goes in the holidays.
Wohin fährst du normalerweise in Urlaub?

a Ask how long your friend stays there.
b Ask with whom your friend goes on holiday.
c Ask what your friend does on holiday.
d Ask what your friend does in the evenings.
e Ask where your friend went on holiday last year.
(*Notice the change to refer to the past tense.*)
f Ask how your friend travelled there.
g Ask what the weather was like.
h Ask what your friend did there.
i Ask what your friend is going to do next summer.
(*Notice the change to refer to the future.*)

2 Now complete the role-play below. Practise the role-play with your partner, taking it in turns to ask and answer the questions.

Exam Tip
- In this role-play below, you have to ask three questions. This shows how important it is for you to learn both the questions and the answers in your list of phrases.

Teacher's Role

1 Wie schön, dass du wieder hier bist.
2 Ich bin mit meinen Freunden in die Berge gefahren.
3 Nicht schlecht.
4 Wir sind oft in die Stadt gegangen. Was machst du gern in den Ferien? Warum?
5 Du hast Recht.

Candidate's Role

You are talking to your German friend about your holidays.
1 Ask where your friend went last year.
2 Ask what the weather was like.
3 Ask what your friend did in the evenings.
4 !

Your teacher will play the part of your friend and will speak first.

(Adapted from AQA/NEAB)

Tourism

Higher Tier H

Im Verkehrsamt
Haben Sie eine Broschüre über die Weinberge?
Wie ist das Wetter im Herbst?
Wir möchten eine Ferienwohnung mieten.
Gibt es eine Pauschalreise nach Griechenland?

Meinungen äußern
Wohin sollen wir diesen Winter in Urlaub fahren?
Ich möchte gern in eine Großstadt fahren.
Ich möchte gern in die Berge fahren.
Ich möchte lieber an die See fahren.
Ich war noch nie in den USA.
Fahren wir dorthin!
Ich war schon einmal dort. Es hat mir nicht sehr gut gefallen.
Ich schwimme sehr gern.
Das Wasser soll schön warm sein.
Ich interessiere mich für Kunst.
Gibt es eine Kunstgalerie in der Stadt?
Ich möchte am liebsten den Dom besichtigen.
Ich möchte lieber die Altstadt besuchen.
Das wäre schön.
Ich möchte lieber in einem Hotel wohnen, weil es hier oft regnet.
Ich möchte nicht segeln.
Es ist gefährlich und ich kann nicht gut schwimmen.

Die Ferien
Wann fangen deine Ferien an und wann hören sie auf?
Mein Urlaub in Spanien hat mir so gut gefallen, weil das Wetter so schön war.
Es war mir in Griechenland viel zu heiß.
Wir haben die Ruinen besichtigt, aber wir waren etwas enttäuscht.
Es war voller Touristen.
Nachts konnten wir nicht schlafen, weil es so heiß war.
Wohin fährst du nächstes Jahr?
Ich möchte nächstes Jahr nach Österreich fahren.
Wir bleiben lieber in England, weil uns das Essen im Ausland nicht gut schmeckt.

In the tourist office
Have you got a brochure on the vineyards?
What is the weather like in the autumn?
We would like to rent a holiday apartment.
Is there a package tour to Greece?

Expressing opinions
Where should we go on holiday this winter?
I would like to go to a city.
I would like to go into the mountains.
I would prefer to go to the sea.
I have never been to the U.S.A.
Let's go there!
I've already been there. I didn't like it very much.
I like swimming very much.
The water is supposed to be lovely and warm.
I am interested in art.
Is there an art gallery in the town?
Most of all I'd like to see the cathedral.
I would prefer to visit the old town.
That would be lovely.
I would prefer to stay in a hotel because it often rains here.
I don't want to go sailing.
It is dangerous and I can't swim well.

Holidays
When do your holidays start and when do they end?
I liked my holiday in Spain so much
because the weather was so lovely.
It was far too hot for me in Greece.
We visited the ruins but we were a bit disappointed.
It was full of tourists.
We couldn't sleep at night because it was so hot.
Where are you going next year?
I'd like to go to Austria next year.
We prefer to stay in England because we don't like the food abroad.

Du machst Pläne für deinen nächsten Urlaub.

1. Wohin sollen wir diesen Sommer in Urlaub fahren?
   — Ich war noch nie in Griechenland. Fahren wir dorthin?

2. Warum möchtest du dorthin fahren?
   — Ich möchte die alten Ruinen besichtigen und ich möchte mich am Strand sonnen.

3. Ich war schon einmal dort und es war mir im Sommer zu heiß.
   — Was möchtest du denn machen?

4. Ich möchte gern nach New York fahren.
   — Ach, schrecklich! Die Großstädte sind immer so laut und so voll.

5. Also, fahren wir in die Berge?
   — Ja, das wäre auch schön. Ich wandere sehr gern.

6. Und man kann auch in den Seen schwimmen.
   — Abgemacht! Was für Pauschalreisen gibt es in der Broschüre?

Practise the dialogue with your partner until you can reproduce it using only the cue words below.
a Wo? **b** Grund **c** Alternative **d** New York **e** Berge **f** Meinung

64

Higher Tier H

Exam Practice

A

1 Re-write the cartoon dialogue on the previous page to match these instructions:

You and your German friend are discussing where to go on holiday this winter. You want to lie in the sun somewhere. Your friend wants to visit London. You both enjoy sport, especially skiing.

2 In your Higher Tier role-play, you will usually have to state an opinion. Whenever you do this make sure that you follow your opinion with a reason. Complete the sentences below by adding a reason.

Example: Ich fahre lieber ins Ausland, weil *das Wetter dort schöner ist.*

   a Ich verbringe meine Ferien am liebsten in England, weil …
   b Nächstes Jahr möchte ich an die See fahren, weil …
   c Ich wohne gern in einer Ferienwohnung, weil …
   d Ich wohne lieber auf einem Campingplatz, weil …
   e Das Hotel hat mir nicht gut gefallen, weil …

B

> *Exam Tip*
> - In this topic, you must be prepared to discuss different types of holiday to decide which to choose. Do not expect the teacher always to agree. Be ready to negotiate.
> - Always, give a reason for your choice.
> - Always, prepare a second choice with a reason, to offer your teacher an alternative.
> - You can use the topic and role-play situation to prepare for the ! task, but you must listen very carefully to the question and be flexible when answering it, even if it is not the question you prepared.
> - Likewise, you can also use the cues to prepare your answers, but you must always listen really carefully to your teacher's questions: they may not be what you expected.

1 Cover the teacher's role. Take just four minutes to prepare the candidate's role below.
2 Now read the teacher's role. Check your answers and write out the whole dialogue.

Teacher's Role

1 Ich weiß nicht, welchen Urlaub ich lieber habe. Was meinst du? Warum? *(Candidate's task: to state preference and reason.)*
2a *Candidate chooses Austrian holiday:* Ich glaube, ich fahre lieber an die Nordseeküste. Wie gefällt dir Segeln?
2b *Candidate chooses North Sea holiday:* Ich glaube ich fahre lieber nach Österreich. Wie gefällt dir Wandern? *(Candidate's task: to express an opinion about the activity mentioned.)*
3 Du hast Recht. Wie bekommst du das Geld für den Urlaub? *(Candidate's task: to explain how the money for the holiday will be saved.)*
4 Wann fangen deine Sommerferien an und wann hören sie auf? *(Candidate's task: to give details of holiday dates.)*
5 Schön. Dann rufe ich an und nehme eine Reservierung vor.

Candidate's Role

You and your German friend are saving for a holiday together. You have reduced the choice to the two below.

a Österreich
  Campingplatz
  Berge
  Ruhe, Wandern
  10 Tage DM 300

b Nordseeküste
  Hotel
  Strand
  Sonne, Discos, Segeln
  1 Woche DM 450

1 *Meinung*
2 *!*
3 *Geld*
4 *Ferientermine*

Your teacher will play the part of your German friend and will speak first.

(AQA/NEAB Short Course – 1998)

Accommodation

Foundation Tier & Foundation/Higher Tier F&F/H

Zimmer reservieren / Reserving rooms

Haben Sie ein Zimmer frei?	Have you got a room free?
Ich möchte ein Doppelzimmer mit Dusche reservieren.	I would like to reserve a double room with a shower.
Haben Sie ein Einzelzimmer mit Bad frei?	Have you got a single room with a bath free?
Ist das Zimmer mit Dusche?	Has the room got a shower?
Für wann möchten Sie das Zimmer?	When would you like the room for?
Vom ersten bis zum dritten Mai.	From the 1st to the 3rd of May.
Haben Sie ein Zimmer für heute Abend frei?	Have you got a room free for tonight?
Für wie viele Nächte?	For how many nights?
Für eine Nacht.	For one night.
Was kostet das Zimmer pro Nacht?	What does the room cost per night?
Ist das inklusive Frühstück? Was kostet Vollpension?	Is breakfast included? What does full board cost?
Ich nehme das Zimmer.	I'll take the room.
Das ist zu teuer.	It is too expensive.
Haben Sie ein Zimmer ohne Dusche?	Have you got a room without a shower?
Gibt es ein anderes Hotel in der Nähe?	Is there another hotel nearby?

Im Hotel / In the hotel

Haben Sie schon reserviert?	Have you already reserved (a room)?
Ich habe für heute Abend ein Zimmer reserviert.	I have reserved a room for tonight.
Ihr Name, bitte?	Your name, please?
Mein Name ist Smith.	My name is Smith.
Wo ist das Restaurant? Wo sind die Toiletten?	Where is the restaurant? Where are the toilets?
Gibt es einen Kinderspielplatz?	Is there a playground for children?
Wann ist Frühstück?	When is breakfast?
Kann ich hier zu Abend essen?	Can I get an evening meal here?
Ich möchte meinen Schlüssel, bitte. Zimmer Nummer vierzig.	I would like my key, please. Room number 40.
Ich möchte bezahlen, bitte. Die Rechnung, bitte.	I would like to pay, please. The bill, please.

Unterkunft finden / Finding accommodation

Was kostet es für eine Woche für einen Wohnwagen?	What does it cost for a week for a caravan?
Wo kann ich hier übernachten?	Where can I stay the night here?
Gibt es eine Jugendherberge in der Nähe?	Is there a youth hostel nearby?
Haben Sie Platz für ein Zelt für morgen Abend?	Have you got room for a tent for tomorrow evening?
Ich habe einen Platz für ein Zelt reserviert.	I have reserved a place for a tent.

Du möchtest ein Zimmer reservieren. Du rufst das Hotel an.

A
- Hotel Krone. Guten Abend.
- Was für ein Zimmer möchten Sie?
- Und für wie viele Nächte möchten Sie das Zimmer?

Du kommst im Hotel an.

B
- Guten Abend. Haben Sie schon reserviert?
- Ihr Name, bitte.
- Könnten Sie Ihren Namen bitte buchstabieren?

1 Complete the dialogues above with a partner, taking turns to play the two roles. You must spell your name quickly and without hesitation. This is really important for your exam.
2 Now adapt the dialogues to book a double room with a shower from January 16th to January 20th.

Foundation Tier & Foundation/Higher Tier F&F/H

Exam Practice

F A

1. Get a partner to test you on all the phrases on the previous page.
2. Without looking at the phrases, ask the questions below in German. (In your Foundation Tier role-play you will have to ask at least one question.)
   a Ask if the hotel has a room available.
   b Ask if the hotel has a restaurant.
   c Ask if there is a playground for children.
   d Ask when breakfast is served.
   e Ask for your key to room 240.
   f Ask what full board costs.
   g Ask for the bill.
   h Ask if there is another hotel nearby.
3. Again, without looking at the phrases on the previous page, complete the role-play below.

Exam Tip
- Keep your answers short and simple. Be prepared again to give your name and spell it.

Teacher's Role

Du kommst in einem Hotel an. Ich arbeite in dem Hotel.
1 Guten Tag. Bitte sehr?
2 Für wie viele Nächte?
3 Ist in Ordnung.
4 Alle Zimmer sind mit Bad.
5 Vierzig Mark pro Nacht.

Candidate's Role

You go to a hotel in Germany.
1 Say you want to book a single room.
2 Say you want to stay for two nights.
3 Ask if the room has a bath or shower.
4 Ask how much it costs.

Your teacher will play the part of the person working in the hotel and will speak first.

(Adapted from AQA/NEAB – 1998)

F/H B

1. Cover the teacher's role on the left and, in three minutes only, prepare the candidate's role.
2. Look at the teacher's role and practise the conversation with a partner. Continue until you can both play the client's role perfectly.

Exam Tip
- In this role-play, you have to give a reason for changing your booking. This is a task you may not expect. In your Foundation/Higher Tier role-play, it may sometimes be difficult to predict what your teacher will ask you for the ! task. If this is the case, listen very carefully to your teacher's question. Don't panic. Think of the simplest answer you can, and one you can say easily in German, and you will score good marks, e.g. *Ich muss zu Hause bleiben* or *Ich bin krank*.

Teacher's Role

1 Campingplatz Hirsch. Guten Tag.
2 Und wie kann ich Ihnen helfen?
3 Gibt es ein Problem?
4 Warum?
5 Ist in Ordnung.

Candidate's Role

You telephone the owner of a German campsite.
1 Tell him/her who you are and where you are phoning from.
2 Tell him/her when your reservation is for and for how long.
3 Ask him/her if you can come two weeks later.
4 !

Your teacher will play the part of the campsite owner and will speak first.

(AQA/NEAB – 1998)

67

Accommodation

Higher Tier H

Am Campingplatz
Wir brauchen einen Platz für ein großes Zelt.
Wir möchten einen Platz in der Nähe der Duschen.
Wir möchten einen Platz im Schatten.
Wo kann man hier einkaufen?
Gibt es noch einen Campingplatz in der Nähe?

At the campsite
We need a place for a large tent.
We would like a place near the showers.
We would like a place in the shade.
Where can we shop here?
Is there another campsite nearby?

In der Jugendherberge
Haben Sie Platz für zwei Erwachsene und zwei Kinder?
Leider haben wir keinen Platz mehr frei.
Wann macht die Jugendherberge zu?
Können wir Bettwäsche leihen?
Ich brauche keine Bettwäsche.
Ich habe meinen eigenen Schlafsack.

In the youth hostel
Have you got room for two adults and two children?
Unfortunately, we have no more room available.
When does the youth hostel close?
Can we hire bed linen?
I don't need any bed linen.
I've got my own sleeping bag.

Unterkunft finden
Ich möchte Ihre Ferienwohnung für eine Woche im August mieten.
Wie groß ist die Wohnung?
Was für Zimmer hat die Wohnung?
Wie ist die Küche ausgestattet?

Finding accommodation
I would like to rent your holiday apartment for one week in August.
How big is the apartment?
What sort of rooms has the apartment got?
How is the kitchen equipped?

Probleme lösen
Wo liegt das Problem genau?
Ich habe kein warmes Wasser im Zimmer.
Der Fernseher funktioniert nicht richtig.
Die Heizung im Zimmer funktioniert nicht.
Ich möchte in ein anderes Zimmer umziehen.
Ich möchte mein Zimmer wechseln.
Ich kann wegen des Lärms nicht schlafen.
Ich kann nicht im Zimmer bleiben, weil es so kalt ist.
Ich muss heute in ein anderes Zimmer umziehen.
Ich kann nicht länger in diesem Zimmer bleiben.
Wir haben keine Zimmer mehr frei.
Ich habe erst ab morgen Zimmer frei.
Gibt es ein anderes Hotel in der Nähe?
Wir wollten um achtzehn Uhr ankommen.
Wir werden nicht vor zwanzig Uhr ankommen.
Wir werden spät ankommen. Unser Schiff hatte Verspätung.
Es gab einen Unfall auf der Autobahn.
Können wir noch zu Abend essen, wenn wir ankommen?
Wir sollen gegen neunzehn Uhr ankommen.

Solving problems
What exactly is wrong?
I have no hot water in the room.
The television isn't working properly.
The heating in the room isn't working.
I would like to move into another room.
I would like to change my room.
I can't sleep because of the noise.
I can't stay in the room because it is so cold.
I must move into another room today.
I can't stay in this room any longer.
We have no more rooms available.
I've only got rooms available from tomorrow.
Is there another hotel nearby?
We were to arrive at 6 p.m.
We will not arrive before 8 p.m.
We will be arriving late. Our ship was late.
There was an accident on the motorway.
Can we still have dinner when we arrive?
We should arrive at about 7 p.m.

Du wohnst in einem Hotel in Deutschland. Leider gibt es Probleme mit deinem Zimmer.

Panel 1: Wie kann ich Ihnen helfen?
Panel 2: Das tut mir Leid. Was möchten Sie machen?
Panel 3: Leider haben wir keine Zimmer mehr frei.

1. Write out the dialogue in full. What must the woman say in the last picture to convince the manager to change her room?
2. Write a new dialogue with your partner. This time the shower does not work, there is no hot water and the room is very noisy! The guest must insist on another room as soon as possible.
3. Finally, create and act out your own dialogue. Decide what is wrong with the room and what you want the manager to do. Can the rest of the class find out what your problems are?

Higher Tier H

Exam Practice

1. Make sure you know all the phrases on pages 66 and 68. Work with a partner and test each other on the phrases. Make sure you always ask your partner to translate from English into German and test the phrases in random order. You will learn them better that way.
2. Cover the teacher's role and prepare the candidate's role in just four minutes.
3. Now read the teacher's role. Check your answers and practise the whole dialogue with your partner. Write out the completed dialogue.

> *Exam Tip*
> - Listen very carefully to what your teacher says and be ready to be flexible in your answers.
> - Answer in detail, with no ambiguity and no mistakes.
>
> When you are preparing your role-plays, look for:
> - tasks defined for you in the introduction;
> - tasks where you are free to say what you want;
> - tasks where you may need to explain or justify something
> - how many details you need to give (aiming always to give at least two details.)

Teacher's Role

1. Schmidt. Guten Tag. *(Candidate's task: to say why he/she is telephoning.)*
2. Wann möchten Sie genau kommen? *(Candidate's task: to respond, giving dates.)*
3. Kein Problem. Was möchten Sie reservieren? *(Candidate's task: to make the booking, giving number of people and other requirements.)*
4. Ist in Ordnung. Und was möchten Sie während Ihres Aufenthalts machen? *(Candidate's task: to say what he/she intends to do.)*
5. Gute Idee!

Candidate's Role

Your family wants to rent an apartment in Germany during the winter holidays. You telephone the owner to make a booking.

1. *Anruf – warum?*
2. *Termine*
3. *Details der Reservierung*
4. *!*

Your teacher will play the part of the apartment owner and will speak first.

(Adapted from AQA/NEAB Short Course – 1998)

> *Exam Tip*
> **Working with the cues**
>
> The cues in this role-play should have been quite helpful. How well did you predict what the teacher was going to ask you? Look at the cues again.
>
> 1. *Anruf – warum?* links closely with the introduction, so you can be in control of what you say. You should say who you are, where you are phoning from and why.
> 2. *Termine* tells you that you must give details of dates.
> 3. *Details der Reservierung* is less clear. You can prepare details, but you must be ready to answer other questions your teacher could ask, e.g.
>   a *Wie viele sind Sie denn?*
>   b *Was für eine Wohnung möchten Sie genau?*
>   c *Wo möchten Sie die Wohnung?*
>   d *Wie viele Schlafzimmer brauchen Sie?*
>   e *Haben Sie besondere Wünsche?*
> 4. *!* – This could be any of the questions below. Work with a partner and practise asking and answering these questions. (Remember to give at least two details in each answer.)
>   a *Wann kommen Sie genau an?*   e *Waren Sie schon früher hier?*
>   b *Wie kommen Sie hierher?*   f *Was machen Sie gern?*
>   c *Brauchen Sie etwas in der Wohnung?*   g *Was für Ausflüge möchten Sie machen?*
>   d *Warum haben Sie diese Wohnung ausgewählt?*   h *Wo machen Sie normalerweise Ihre Ferien?*

Exam Practice for the Foundation Tier

Here are some Foundation Tier role-plays which have been set at GCSE. Practise them until you find them easy.
1 Revise the useful phrases suggested before each role-play.
2 Cover the teacher's role and prepare the candidate's role in three minutes.
3 Look at the teacher's role and, with a partner, practise the role-play.

> *Exam Tip*
> - Read the instructions carefully and prepare exactly what they say.
> - Decide whether you will use *du* or *Sie*.
> - If the instructions tell you to say that <u>you want</u> or <u>you would like</u>, you must say *ich möchte*. If you have to say that <u>you like</u> something, you should say *ich mag* or use a verb with *gern*.
> - Use the German that you have learnt in this book and keep it short and simple.

A
Revise page 26 before you do this role-play.

Teacher's Role

Dein deutscher Gast ist gerade angekommen. Ich bin der Gast.
1 Grüß dich. Ich bin der Stefan/die Steffi.
2 Danke schön.
3 Guten Tag. Freut mich!
4 Danke.
5 Ja, bitte.

Candidate's Role

A German friend arrives at your house.

1 Invite your friend in.
2 Introduce your sister.
3 Offer your friend a seat.
4 Ask your friend if he/she wants something to drink.

Your teacher will play the part of your friend and will speak first.

(AQA/NEAB – 1997)

B
Revise pages 26 and 30 before you do this role-play.

Teacher's Role

Du sprichst mit deinem deutschen Freund/deiner deutschen Freundin. Ich bin der Freund/die Freundin.
1 Wie viel Taschengeld bekommst du?
2 Hast du einen Job?
3 Aha! Wie alt ist sie?
4 Was machen wir heute Abend?
5 Toll.

Candidate's Role

You are talking to your German friend about pocket money.
1 Say you don't get pocket money.
2 Say you help your grandmother.
3 Say your grandmother is 70 next year.
4 Ask your friend to go to the cinema.

Your teacher will play the part of your friend and will speak first.

(AQA/NEAB – 1998)

Foundation Tier **F**

C
Revise pages 30 and 58 before you do this role-play.

Teacher's Role
Du sprichst mit deinem deutschen Freund/deiner deutschen Freundin. Ich bin der Freund/die Freundin.
1 Wo arbeitest du samstags?
2 Wie viel Geld verdienst du?
3 Was machst du mit dem Geld?
4 Du hast aber Glück!
5 Ja, ich mag Musik sehr.

Candidate's Role
You are talking to your German friend about work.

1 Say you work in a factory.
2 Say you earn £12 a day.
3 Say you buy cassettes with the money.
4 Ask if your friend likes music.

Your teacher will play the part of your friend and will speak first.

(Adapted from AQA/NEAB – 1998)

D
Revise pages 8 and 58 before you do this role-play.

Teacher's Role
Du sprichst mit deinem deutschen Freund/deiner deutschen Freundin. Ich bin der Freund/die Freundin.
1 Was ist dein Lieblingsfach?
2 Warum?
3 Du hast Glück.
4 Nicht besonders. Es ist schwer.
5 Ich wünsche dir viel Glück!

Candidate's Role
You are talking to your German friend about school.

1 Say you like Geography.
2 Say the teacher is interesting.
3 Ask if your friend likes English.
4 Say you want to do Geography and English next year.

Your teacher will play the part of your friend and will speak first.

(Adapted from AQA/NEAB – 1998)

E
Revise pages 30 and 34 before you do this role-play.

Teacher's Role
Du sprichst mit deinem deutschen Freund/deiner deutschen Freundin. Ich bin der Freund/die Freundin.
1 Was für Sendungen siehst du gern?
2 Was für Filme?
3 Siehst du oft fern?
4 Das ist nicht viel.
5 Ja.

Candidate's Role
You are watching television with your German friend.

1 Say you like films.
2 Say you prefer comedies.
3 Say you watch television for 10 hours a week.
4 Ask your friend if there is a lot of sport on television in Germany.

Your teacher will play the part of your friend and will speak first.

(Adapted from AQA/NEAB – 1998)

Exam Practice for the Foundation/Higher Tier

Here are some role-plays which have been set at Foundation/Higher Tier. Practise them, on your own and with a partner, until you are word perfect.
1. Revise the useful phrases on the pages suggested before each role-play.
2. Cover the teacher's role and prepare the candidate's role in four minutes.
3. Look at the teacher's role and, with a partner, practise the role-play.

Exam Tip
- Read the instructions carefully and prepare what you can. However, remember that you must listen carefully to your teacher's questions.
- Give *all* the information in each task and any additional information your teacher asks for.
- In your answers, always try to use a verb or give *two* details.
- Try not to look up any words, but rather use the German you know.
- Make sure that you can spell your name and the name of the town where you live, as well as the names of your family and friends (see page 7).

A
Revise pages 12, 14 and 30 before you do this role-play.

Exam Tip
- Remember to give *two* activities for task 4.

Teacher's Role

1. Wo wohnst du?
2. Wie ist dein Haus?
3. Wie hilfst du zu Hause?
4. Ich auch. Was machst du in deiner Freizeit?
5. Schön.

Candidate's Role

You are talking to your German friend about where you live.
1. Tell him/her that you live in a house on the edge of town.
2. Tell him/her that your house is quite big with four bedrooms.
3. Tell him/her that you make your bed and tidy your room.
4. !

Your teacher will play the part of your friend and will speak first.

(Adapted from AQA/NEAB – 1998)

B
Revise page 54 before you do this role-play.

Teacher's Role

1. Bitte sehr?
2. Sonst noch etwas?
3. Der Zug fährt direkt nach Bonn.
4. Wie ist Ihr Familienname? Wie schreibt man das, bitte?
5. Danke schön.

Candidate's Role

You are at a train station in Germany.
1. Ask for a return ticket to Bonn.
2. Ask where you must change.
3. Reserve a seat in a non-smoker.
4. !

Your teacher will play the part of the ticket clerk and will speak first.

(AQA/NEAB – 1998)

Foundation/Higher Tier F/H

C
Revise pages 30 and 58 before you do this role-play.

Exam Tip
Remember to give *two* activities for task 4. You can use exactly the same answer as for task 4 in **A**!

Teacher's Role

1 Warum arbeiten Sie hier in Koblenz?
2 Was machen Sie hier im Restaurant?
3 Wie viele Stunden arbeiten Sie am Tag?
4 Was machen Sie, wenn Sie nicht arbeiten?
5 Ich wünsche Ihnen viel Spaß!

Candidate's Role

You are working in a restaurant in Koblenz. A customer asks about you and your work.
1 Tell him/her that you are here to learn German.
2 Tell him/her what you do in the restaurant.
3 Tell him/her how long you work each day.
4 !

Your teacher will play the part of the customer and will speak first.

(AQA/NEAB – 1997)

D
Revise page 30 before you do this role-play.

Exam Tip
• Remember to give *two* activities for the last task. Again, this is a very similar question to the unexpected question in role-plays **A** and **C**. You may even be able to use the same answer again!

Teacher's Role

1 Was möchtest du heute Abend machen?
2 Ich gehe in den Jugendklub in der Stadt.
3 Man kann Verschiedenes machen.
4 Es geht. Was machst du normalerweise abends?
5 Ich bleibe gewöhnlich zu Hause.

Candidate's Role

You are discussing what to do this evening with your German friend.
1 Ask if your friend is a member of a club.
2 Ask what there is to do there.
3 Ask what he/she thinks of the club.
4 !

Your teacher will play the part of the friend and will speak first.

(Adapted from AQA/NEAB – 1997)

E
Revise pages 26 and 58 before you do this role-play.

Exam Tip
Remember to give *two* activities for task 4. This time you are talking about what someone else does, so your verb must end in **-t**.

Teacher's Role

1 Hast du viele Geschwister?
2 Wie sieht dein Bruder aus?
3 Was ist er von Beruf?
4 Und was macht er in seiner Freizeit?
5 Ich treibe gern Sport.

Candidate's Role

You have met a German boy/girl at the disco.
1 Tell him/her you have a brother and two sisters.
2 Describe your brother's hair and eyes.
3 Tell him/her what your brother does for a living.
4 !

Your teacher will play the part of the German boy/girl and will speak first.

(Adapted from AQA/NEAB – 1998)

Exam Practice for the Higher Tier

Here are some role-plays which have been set at Higher Tier at GCSE. Practise them until you feel confident that you could cope with a role-play like this in your exam.

1. Revise the useful phrases on the pages suggested before each role-play.
2. Cover the teacher's role and prepare the candidate's role in four minutes.
3. Look at the teacher's role and, with a partner, practise the role-play. Read carefully the notes in brackets in the teacher's role. These show you what you need to do to score full marks.

Exam Tip
- Read the instructions carefully. Sometimes, important instructions are given in the English introduction. Make sure you include these details in your answers.
- To score the full four marks for each task, you must complete each task in detail. Remember that it is not easy to predict exactly what you have to say, so you must be flexible enough to answer the question your teacher asks even if it is not the question you prepared. You must therefore listen very carefully to what your teacher says.
- Whenever you are asked to describe something, give at least two details.
- Whenever you are asked to make a suggestion or express an opinion, you must always follow it with a reason.
- Be prepared to negotiate. If you are planning an activity always suggest an alternative activity or another time or place.
- Be prepared to spell your name and address and to give your telephone number including the dialling code.
- Be prepared for a mixture of topics. Examiners often combine more than one topic in a role-play.
- Keep your answers detailed but simple. Use the German you know.

A
Revise page 68 before you do this role-play.

Teacher's Role
1. Wie kann ich Ihnen helfen? *(Candidate's task: to say that he/she wants to change his/her room.)*
2. Wo liegt das Problem genau? *(Candidate's task: to explain the problem.)*
3. Es tut mir Leid. Ich schicke morgen früh jemanden hinauf. Geht das? *(Candidate's task: to reject the manager's suggestion and insist on a solution today.)*
4. Ach, das ist ein Problem. Wir haben heute keine Zimmer mehr frei. Was möchten Sie machen? *(Candidate's task: to say what he/she wants to do.)*
5. Einen Augenblick, bitte.

Candidate's Role
You have just booked into a hotel in Germany but there is a problem with your room. You want to change your room today and go to see the manager.
1. *Grund*
2. *Details des Problems*
3. *Vorschlag der Hotelleitung*
4. *!*

Your teacher will play the part of the hotel manager and will speak first.

(Adapted from AQA/NEAB – 1998)

B
Revise page 32 before you do this role-play.

Teacher's Role
1. Was kann ich machen, um fit zu werden? *(Candidate's task: to suggest a suitable sport.)*
2. Das mag ich nicht. Warum machst du das gern? *(Candidate's task: to say why he/she likes that sport.)*
3. Also, wann kann man das machen? *(Candidate's task: to say when it is possible to play – two details needed.)*
4. Das möchte ich nicht. Was können wir sonst zusammen machen? Wann können wir es machen? *(Candidate's task: to suggest a sport to do together and to say when.)*
5. In Ordnung. Machen wir das.

Candidate's Role
You and your German friend are discussing sporting activities.
1. *Welcher Sport*
2. *Warum*
3. *!*
4. *Vorschlag*

Your teacher will play the part of your friend and will speak first.

(Adapted from AQA/NEAB – 1998)

Higher Tier H

> *Exam Tip*
> - The third task is quite difficult. Think of something which you know in German, e.g. *Können Sie die Polizei anrufen?*

C
Revise page 52 before you do this role-play.

Teacher's Role

1 Wie kann ich Ihnen helfen? *(Candidate's task: to say his/her bag has gone missing.)*
2 Wo haben Sie die Tasche schon gesucht? *(Candidate's task: to say where he/she has looked for it – two details needed.)*
3 Also, was kann ich für Sie tun? *(Candidate's task: to suggest what's to be done.)*
4 Kein Problem. Können Sie die Tasche und den Inhalt bitte beschreiben? *(Candidate's task: to give a full description of the bag and its contents.)*
5 Einen Augenblick, bitte.

Candidate's Role

You are staying in a hotel in Austria when you discover that your bag is missing from your room. You speak to the hotel manager.
1 *Problem*
2 *Wo*
3 *Vorschlag*
4 *!*

Your teacher will play the part of the hotel manager and will speak first.

(AQA/NEAB – 1998)

D
Revise page 20 and 56 before you do this role-play.

Teacher's Role

1 Was fehlt Ihnen? *(Candidate's task: to describe his/her symptoms – two details needed.)*
2 Was ist mit Ihnen passiert? *(Candidate's task: to say he/she has had an accident.)*
3 Wo und wann ist das passiert? *(Candidate's task: to say where and when it happened.)*
4 Wen soll ich anrufen? Wie ist die Telefonnummer? *(Candidate's task: to say who can be contacted and to give a telephone number.)*
5 Ich rufe jetzt an.

Candidate's Role

You have had an accident in Germany and go to the hospital.
1 *Problem*
2 *Unfall*
3 *Wo und wann*
4 *!*

Your teacher will play the part of the doctor and will speak first.

(Adapted from AQA/NEAB – 1998)

E
Revise pages 26, 34, 46 and 52 before you do this role-play.

Teacher's Role

1 Wie kann ich Ihnen helfen? *(Candidate's task: to say that he/she cannot find his/her German friend.)*
2 Wo und wann wollten Sie sich treffen? *(Candidate's task: to say where and when they had arranged to meet.)*
3 Welche Kleidung trägt Ihr Freund/Ihre Freundin? *(Candidate's task: to describe the clothes of the German friend – three details needed.)*
4 Und wie sieht er/sie aus? *(Candidate's task: to say what the friend looks like – three details needed.)*
5 Einen Augenblick, bitte.

Candidate's Role

You arrive at a station in Germany and find that your German friend is not there to meet you. You go to the Information Desk.
1 *Problem*
2 *Wo und wann*
3 *Kleidung*
4 *!*

Your teacher will play the part of the clerk and will speak first.

(Adapted from AQA/NEAB – 1998)

Numbers & Days

Die Zahlen

eins	one	*erste*	first
zwei	two	*zweite*	second
drei	three	*dritte*	third
vier	four	*vierte*	fourth
fünf	five	*fünfte*	fifth
sechs	six	*sechste*	sixth
sieben	seven	*siebte*	seventh
acht	eight	*achte*	eighth
neun	nine	*neunte*	ninth
zehn	ten	*zehnte*	tenth
elf	eleven	*elfte*	eleventh
zwölf	twelve	*zwölfte*	twelfth
dreizehn	thirteen	*dreizehnte*	thirteenth
vierzehn	fourteen	*vierzehnte*	fourteenth
fünfzehn	fifteen	*fünfzehnte*	fifteenth
sechzehn	sixteen	*sechzehnte*	sixteenth
siebzehn	seventeen	*siebzehnte*	seventeenth
achtzehn	eighteen	*achtzehnte*	eighteenth
neunzehn	nineteen	*neunzehnte*	nineteenth
zwanzig	twenty	*zwanzigste*	twentieth
einundzwanzig	twenty-one	*einundzwanzigste*	twenty-first
zweiundzwanzig	twenty-two	*zweiundzwanzigste*	twenty-second
dreißig	thirty	*dreißigste*	thirtieth
vierzig	forty		
fünfzig	fifty		
sechzig	sixty		
siebzig	seventy		
achtzig	eighty		
neunzig	ninety		
hundert	one hundred		
hunderteins	one hundred and one		
zweihundert	two hundred		
tausend	one thousand		

Die Uhrzeit

Es ist ein Uhr.	It is one o'clock.
Um zwei Uhr	At two o'clock
Um dreizehn Uhr	At 13.00 (1 p.m.)
Um achtzehn Uhr	At 18.00 (6 p.m.)
Um zehn Uhr fünf	At 10.05
Um sieben Uhr fünfzehn	At 7.15
Um elf Uhr dreißig	At 11.30
Um zwölf Uhr fünfundvierzig	At 12.45
Um Viertel nach eins	At a quarter past one
Um Viertel vor neun	At a quarter to nine
Um zehn nach zwei	At ten past two
Um fünfundzwanzig vor drei	At twenty-five to three
Um halb sechs	At half past five
Um halb zwölf	At half past eleven
Um halb eins	At half past twelve

Die Wochentage

Montag	Monday
Dienstag	Tuesday
Mittwoch	Wednesday
Donnerstag	Thursday
Freitag	Friday
Samstag	Saturday
Sonntag	Sunday

Months, Date & Question Words

Die Monate

Januar	January
Februar	February
März	March
April	April
Mai	May
Juni	June
Juli	July
August	August
September	September
Oktober	October
November	November
Dezember	December

Das Datum

am dritten August	on August 3rd
neunzehnhundertneunundneunzig	1999
Wir haben heute Montag, den einundzwanzigsten September.	Today is Monday, September 21st.

Question Words

	Was?	**What?**
Was machst du am Wochenende?		What do you do at the weekend?
	Wie?	**How?**
Wie kommst du zur Schule?		How do you get to school?
	Wo?	**Where?**
Wo treffen wir uns?		Where shall we meet?
	Wann?	**When?**
Wann kommst du an?		When do you arrive?
	Welcher/welche/welches?	**Which?**
Welchen Ausflug möchtest du lieber machen?		Which excursion would you prefer to do?
	Wer?	**Who?**
Wer kommt mit?		Who is coming with us?
	Mit wem?	**With whom?**
Mit wem fährst du in Urlaub?		With whom do you go on holiday?
	Wie viel?	**How much?**
Wie viel möchten Sie?		How much would you like?
	Wie viele?	**How many?**
Wie viele sind Sie denn?		How many people are you?
	Was für?	**What kind of?**
Was für Eis möchten Sie?		What sort of ice cream would you like?
	Wie lange?	**How long?**
Wie lange möchten Sie hier bleiben?		How long would you like to stay here?
	Warum?	**Why?**
Warum gefällt dir das?		Why do you like it?

Exam Tip
- In your Foundation/Higher Tier role-play and in your Higher Tier role-play you will have to understand and answer your teacher's questions. You will not be able to prepare these questions in advance if they are indicated by a !.
- It is very important to be able to answer the question quickly. To do this you must know the question words really well.

German–English Glossary

This is a list of German words which appear in the book and which are not in the key phrases.

abgemacht	agreed
der/die Angestellte(n)	employee
anrufen	to 'phone
anstrengend	tiring
ärgern	to annoy
auch	also
der Aufenthalt	stay
(auf Video) aufnehmen	to record (on video)
ausgehen	to go out
der Beamte(n)	male official
die Beamtin(nen)	female official
die Beschreibung(en)	description
blass	pale
der Champignon(s)	mushroom
die Einladung(en)	invitation
die Entschuldigung(en)	apology
die Erbse(n)	pea
die Erfahrung(en)	experience
fleißig	hard-working
ich freue mich darauf	I am looking forward to it
das freut mich	I am pleased
die Gegend	region
das Gemüse	vegetable
gemütlich	cosy
genau	exactly
genügen	to satisfy
das Geschäft(e)	shop
die Getränkekarte(n)	drinks menu
der Grund(¨e)	reason
halten von	to think of
heute	today
die Hochzeit(en)	wedding
hoffentlich	hopefully
der Inhalt(¨e)	contents
die Jahreszeit(en)	season
die Kartoffel(n)	potato
kurz	short
leider	unfortunately
die Leitung	management
mähen	to mow
die Mahlzeit(en)	meal
zum ersten Mal	for the first time
die Meinung(en)	opinion
normalerweise	normally
in Ordnung	O.K.
der Rasen(-)	lawn
die Ruhe	quiet, peace
schade	that's a shame
scheinen	to shine
Schlittschuh laufen	to skate
der Schrank(¨e)	cupboard
die Schulferien	school holidays
der Schultag(e)	school day
das Schweinefleisch	pork
segeln	to sail
sonst	otherwise
spannend	exciting
das Spielzeug(e)	toy
der Strand	beach
der Termin(e)	date
der Unfall(¨e)	accident
der Unterschied(e)	difference
die Verabredung(en)	arrangement, appointment
der Verhältnis(se)	relationship
vormittags	in the mornings
der Vorschlag(¨e)	suggestion
während	during
was für?	what kind of?
der Wunsch(¨e)	wish
die Zwiebel(n)	onion

English–German Glossary

actor	der Schauspieler(-)	coat	der Mantel(¨)	funny	komisch
actress	die Schauspielerin(nen)	college of further education	die Fachhochschule(n)	garden	der Garten(¨)
agreed	einverstanden	comprehensive school	die Gesamtschule(n)	geography	Geographie
along	entlang	cool	kühl	to get out (of a vehicle)	aussteigen
Alps	die Alpen	to cook	kochen	girl	das Mädchen(-)
already	schon	cream	die Sahne	glove	der Handschuh(e)
also	auch	crisps	(Kartoffel) Chips	to go out	ausgehen
always	immer	cup	die Tasse(n)	gram	das Gramm
angry	böse	daily	täglich	grammar school	das Gymnasium
to apologise	sich entschuldigen	dance	tanzen	grandad	Opa
approximately	ungefähr	dark	dunkel	grandma	Oma
armchair	der Sessel(-)	daughter	die Tochter(¨)	grandparents	die Großeltern
to ask	fragen	the day after tomorrow	übermorgen	great!	prima!
aunt	die Tante(n)	the day before yesterday	vorgestern	Greece	Griechenland
Austria	Österreich	degree (on thermometer)	der Grad	group	die Gruppe(n)
Austrian (female)	die Österreicherin(nen)	Denmark	Dänemark	gymnasium	die Turnhalle(n)
Austrian (male)	der Österreicher(-)	dictionary	das Wörterbuch(¨er)	gymnastics	Turnen
awful	furchtbar	dirty	schmutzig	half-board	Halbpension
baby	das Baby(s)	dishwasher (machine)	der Geschirrspülautomat	hand	die Hand(¨e)
baby sitter (female)	die Babysitterin(nen)	door	die Tür(en)	ham	der Schinken
baby sitter (male)	der Babysitter(-)	dress	das Kleid(er)	to happen	passieren
back	der Rücken(-)	dry	trocken	happy	glücklich
badminton	Badminton	ear	das Ohr(en)	hard-working	fleißig
Baltic Sea	die Ostsee	Easter	Ostern	headmaster	der Schuldirektor(en)
banana	die Banane(n)	egg	das Ei(er)	headmistress	die Schuldirektorin(nen)
beard	der Bart(¨e)	empty	leer	healthy	gesund
begin	anfangen	to end	enden	high	hoch
behind	hinter	enormous	enorm	to hike	wandern
Belgium	Belgien	enough	genug	hobby	das Hobby(s)
biology	Biologie	everywhere	überall	to go on holiday	in Urlaub fahren
biro	der Kugelschreiber(-)	exactly	genau	to hope	hoffen
blouse	die Bluse(n)	exam	die Prüfung(en)	hopefully	hoffentlich
boat	das Boot(e)	exercise book	das Heft(e)	horse	das Pferd(e)
book	das Buch(¨er)	excursion	der Ausflug(¨e)	hour	die Stunde(n)
boring	langweilig	eye	das Auge(n)	housewife	die Hausfrau(en)
bungalow	der Bungalow(s)	factory	die Fabrik(en)	idea	die Idee(n)
butter	die Butter	family	die Familie(n)	immediately	sofort
cake	der Kuchen(-)	fast	schnell	important	wichtig
cake shop	die Konditorei(en)	festival	das Fest(e)	inhabitant	der Einwohner(-)
camera	der Fotoapparat(e)	a few	ein paar	information technology	Informatik
carrier bag	die Tüte(n)	final (match)	das Endspiel(e)	instrument	das Instrument(e)
cassette	die Kassette(n)	finger	der Finger(e)	to introduce	vorstellen
cassette recorder	der Kassettenrekorder(-)	first name	der Vorname(n)	Italy	Italien
castle	das Schloss(¨er)	fitness centre	das Fitnesszentrum	jewellery	der Schmuck
central heating	die Zentralheizung	to forget	vergessen	juice	der Saft
chair	der Stuhl(¨e)	fork	die Gabel(n)	knife	das Messer(-)
chemistry	Chemie	France	Frankreich	lamp	die Lampe(n)
chemist's	die Drogerie(n)	free	kostenlos	late	spät
chewing gum	der Kaugummi	to freeze	frieren	lazy	faul
church	die Kirche(n)	French (language)	Französisch	to learn	lernen
class trip	die Klassenfahrt(en)	French man	der Franzose(n)	leather	das Leder
classroom	das Klassenzimmer(-)	French woman	die Französin(nen)	lemonade	die Limonade
clean	sauber	fried egg	das Spiegelei(er)	library	die Bibliothek(en)
closed	geschlossen	friendly	freundlich	light	hell
cloudy	wolkig			litre	der Liter
club	der Verein(e)			a lot	viel

79

English–German Glossary

English	German
luggage	das Gepäck
lunch	das Mittagessen
magazine	die Zeitschrift(en)
main station	der Hauptbahnhof(¨e)
man	der Mann(¨er)
mark (at school)	die Note(n)
mechanic (female)	die Mechanikerin(nen)
mechanic (male)	der Mechaniker(–)
member (of a club)	das Mitglied(er)
metre	der Meter(-)
midday	Mittag
middle	die Mitte
money	das Geld
month	der Monat(e)
multi-coloured	bunt
music	die Musik
mustard	der Senf
narrow	eng
never	nie
newspaper	die Zeitung(en)
New Year	das Neujahr
nice	nett
North Sea	die Nordsee
not yet	noch nicht
now	nun
nurse (female)	die Krankenschwester(n)
nurse (male)	der Krankenpfleger(-)
of course	natürlich
open	offen
open-air swimming pool	das Freibad(ër)
to open a book	aufschlagen
opposite	gegenüber
orange juice	der Orangensaft
outskirts	der Stadtrand
parcel	das Paket(e)
park	der Park
pea	die Erbse(n)
pencil	der Bleistift(e)
penfriend (female)	die Brieffreundin(nen)
penfriend (male)	der Brieffreund(e)
pepper	der Pfeffer
to 'phone	telefonieren
photo	das Foto
to take a photo	fotografieren
physics	Physik
pink	rosa
poor	arm
possible	möglich
post card	die Postkarte(n)
potato	die Kartoffel(n)
to prepare	vorbereiten
price	der Preis(e)
probably	wahrscheinlich
pub	das Gasthaus(¨er)
purse	das Portemonnaie(s)
quick, quickly	schnell
rabbit	das Kaninchen(-)
to read	lesen
to be ready	fertig sein
really	wirklich
red	rot
religious education	Religion
to repeat	wiederholen
reservation	die Reservierung(en)
the Rhine	der Rhein
rich	reich
to ride	reiten
right	richtig
ring	der Ring(e)
river	der Fluß(¨sse)
roller skate	der Rollschuh(e)
ruler	das Lineal(e)
salad	der Salat
sausage	die Wurst(¨e)
to save	sparen
school bag	die Mappe(n)
school boy	der Schüler(-)
school girl	die Schülerin(nen)
season	die Jahreszeit(en)
shop	das Geschäft(e)
short	kurz
shut	geschlossen
sight	die Sehenswürdigkeit(en)
to sign	unterschreiben
to sing	singen
singer (female)	die Sängerin(nen)
singer (male)	der Sänger(-)
sixth form	die Oberstufe
skirt	der Rock(¨e)
slow, slowly	langsam
snow	der Schnee
sock	die Socke(n)
sofa	das Sofa(s)
son	der Sohn(¨e)
soon	bald
souvenir	das Souvenir(s)
Spain	Spanien
Spanish	Spanisch
to spell	buchstabieren
sports ground	der Sportplatz(¨e)
sports centre	das Sportzentrum (Sportzentren)
Spring	der Frühling
stadium	das Stadion (Stadien)
stairs	die Treppe(n)
to stay	bleiben
stereo unit	die Stereoanlage(n)
stomach	der Magen
stormy	stürmisch
strong	stark
stupid	dumm
sugar	der Zucker
sun	die Sonne
sun cream	die Sonnencreme
sweet	das Bonbon(s)
sweet	süß
swimming baths	das Schwimmbad(¨er)
Switzerland	die Schweiz
Swiss (female)	die Schweizerin(nen)
Swiss (male)	der Schweizer(-)
tea	der Tee
teacher (female)	die Lehrerin(nen)
teacher (male)	der Lehrer(-)
team	die Mannschaft(en)
technology (school subject)	Werken
to telephone	telefonieren
tennis	Tennis
terrace house	das Reihenhaus(¨er)
terrible	furchtbar
theatre	das Theater(-)
to think	meinen
through	durch
to tidy up	aufräumen
tie	die Krawatte(n)
toothpaste	die Zahnpasta
tram	die Straßenbahn
T-shirt	das T-Shirt(s)
Turkey (country)	die Türkei
twin	der Zwilling(e)
typical	typisch
ugly	hässlich
uncle	der Onkel(-)
underground (railway)	die U-Bahn
to understand	verstehen
U.S.A.	die USA
usually	gewöhnlich
vegetable	das Gemüse
waiter	der Kellner(-)
waitress	die Kellnerin(nen)
walkman	der Walkman(s)
wallet	die Brieftasche(n)
warm	warm
to watch television	fernsehen
weak	schwach
weather	das Wetter
weather forecast	die Wettervorhersage(n)
wet	nass
white	weiß
wide	breit
win	gewinnen
wine	der Wein
wonderful	wunderbar
wrong	falsch
yoghurt	das Joghurt
youth hostel	die Jugendherberge(n)
zoo	der Zoo(s)